SOUTH MIDDLEBOROUGH

SOUTH MIDDLEBOROUGH

A HISTORY

MICHAEL J. MADDIGAN

THE History PRESS

Published by The History Press
Charleston, SC 29403
www.historypress.net

Images are from the author's collection unless otherwise noted.

Front cover, top: South Middleborough cranberry pickers. *Courtesy of Middleborough Historical Association*; *Bottom*: Dura Higgins. *Courtesy of Sharon (Higgins) Cope-Carriere.*

Back cover, top: Square dance, Scout Cabin, South Middleborough. *Courtesy of Michael J. Maddigan*; *Bottom*: Charles E. Hunt. *Courtesy of Middleborough Historical Association.*

First published 2011

Manufactured in the United States

ISBN 978.1.60949.362.2

Library of Congress Cataloging-in-Publication Data

Maddigan, Michael J.
South Middleborough : a history / Michael J. Maddigan.
p. cm.
Includes index.
ISBN 978-1-60949-362-2
1. South Middleboro (Mass.)--History. I. Title.
F74.S738M34 2011
974.4'82--dc23
2011041044

CONTENTS

ACKNOWLEDGEMENTS

This history could not have been written without a number of important sources, particularly the "South Middleboro" column of the *Middleboro Gazette*, which ran for many years in the pages of that newspaper. Also helpful were the numerous articles written about the community by Jennie (Gammons) Phillips Hayden, a remarkable resident who lived in South Middleborough for most of her life and acted as the caretaker of the community's history. Active into her nineties as a newspaper correspondent, Mrs. Hayden was at one time chronicled as the oldest active newspaper correspondent in the nation. Thanks also go to members of the Wilbur family, who for generations were active in the South Middleborough community. Particularly indispensable were the voluminous diaries and journals of Herbert L. Wilber, which were generously donated to the Middleborough Historical Association in 2009 by Alma (Canova) Wilbur. Herbert L. Wilber (who in contrast to the remainder of his family chose to spell his name with an "e") also took many of the original photographs that appear in this volume. I'd especially like to thank Sharon (Higgins) Cope-Carriere for a delightful afternoon spent sifting through photographs of the Wilbur and Higgins families, for her kindness in sharing stories about her father and grandparents and for her generosity in permitting the use of a number of photographs in this history. Special thanks also go to Martha (Williams) Dupuis, whose love for South Middleborough is apparent. I thank her for her support of this project and her assistance with listing

South Middleborough on the National Register of Historic Places. I am pleased that this beautiful image now has the wider audience it deserves. Finally, I am indebted to the Middleborough Historical Association, which generously permitted the use of several photographs from its collections for this history. This history is, in part, a product of the association's resources. I encourage all readers to support the association's mission to preserve the history of Middleborough.

INTRODUCTION

My book should smell of pines.
—Ralph Waldo Emerson, Self-Reliance *(1841)*

South Middleborough, Massachusetts, has always meant white pine trees. The product of the region's sandy soil, white pines have stood for generations bearing witness to the area's historic development. Attractive to the earliest settlers for timber and heating wood, these same trees formed the basis of a late nineteenth- and early twentieth-century lumber industry that made Middleborough the most productive lumber-producing town in the state. Later, when the lumber industry declined, these same trees provided restful and shady roadways for motorists speeding southward, bound for the resorts of Cape Cod. The ubiquitous tree appears in nearly all the photographs of the era. Throughout the community's historical growth, these trees have been present at South Middleborough, watching over its economic development and, at times, becoming a factor in such development.

In 1905, while speaking before a meeting of the South Middleborough Methodist Church, Matthew H. Cushing noted that "the early history of the southerly part of our town has not been well preserved." The present work is an effort to rectify this oversight. One of several historic villages that compose the town of Middleborough, South Middleborough is located near the extreme southeastern corner of Middleborough, adjoining

While the intersection of Spruce and Locust Streets (known historically as Clark's Corner) served as the village center of South Middleborough throughout the 1800s, modern South Middleborough is centered on the opposite end of Locust Street, near where the fire station, church, cemetery and school are all located. This view from the early 1960s shows Wareham Street running from the lower left to the upper right with Locust Street in the center.

Carver, Wareham and Rochester. Historically, the designation "South Middleborough" has been used interchangeably to refer to both the village of South Middleborough, centered on the junction of Locust Street with Spruce and Wareham Streets, and the entire southern portion of the town of Middleborough, an area including Highlands, France, Mad Mare's Neck and Rock. In 1958, this habitual tendency to lump several distinct districts of southern Middleborough under the name South Middleborough was remarked upon by *Middleboro Gazette* editor Lorenzo Wood, who, tongue-in-cheek, wrote:

> *Our objectors* [in South Middleborough and nearby Rock] *point out, all too often, their sacred precincts are referred to by the general public (and perhaps by* The Gazette *itself) as South Middleboro and they wish it understood that there is a clearly defined line between the two communities. However, we could not get the actual metes and bounds, and therefore will have to call upon our complainants when in doubt.*

In this work, it is the history of the *village* of South Middleborough that shall be the focus, though necessarily, adjoining districts—particularly the older settlement of Fresh Meadows—will be mentioned (see map on page 17).

During the Contact (1500–1620) and First (1620–1675) Periods, South Middleborough's native population appears to have been minimal, and English exploration of the area was limited. English settlement first occurred along the west bank of the Weweantic River at an area that came to be known as Fresh Meadows, a few miles east of modern South Middleborough following the division of the South Purchase in the 1690s. The community became a center of Baptist activism within the area (in distinct contrast to the Congregationalist-dominated Middleborough center) and would become the

The historic South Middleborough Methodist Church has long stood at the spiritual and geographic heart of the community. The Methodist Sunday School, Women's Christian Temperance Union, Epworth League, Ladies' Aid Society, Young People's League and Methodist Youth Fellowship were all popular church-sponsored organizations that gave vibrancy and provided sodality to the community. While its influence has waned, the church remains active and is a historic landmark.

home of the Third Baptist Church of Middleborough in the mid-eighteenth century, at which time the locus of settlement came to reside near the present intersection of Spruce and Locust Streets. Denominationally distinct and geographically distant from Middleborough center, South Middleborough would cultivate a historical tradition of independence. Mid-nineteenth-century economic growth followed the arrival of the Cape Cod Branch Railroad in 1848, during which time South Middleborough developed as an agricultural community dominated by the extensive production and milling of white pine lumber.

Later, the decline of lumber milling in the first two decades of the twentieth century would be followed by the community's most significant period of development, a result of the reconstruction of Wareham Street, the village's principal highway, and its designation by the Commonwealth of Massachusetts as Route 28, one of two routes linking Boston with summer resorts on Cape Cod. With the rapid growth in the number of automobiles passing through South Middleborough, the community's economic attention became focused on the provision of goods and services to motorists who passed in large numbers through the village in the years surrounding World War II en route to tourist destinations on Cape Cod. However, the opening of Route 25 (now Route 495), which bypassed South Middleborough in 1966, brought with it new challenges, not the least of which was the removal of the community's economic base. Since that period, South Middleborough has sometimes struggled to retain its identity as a community of residences and small-scale business enterprises, yet one thing has remained as constant as the pine trees that stand watch over the community: South Middleborough's historic tradition as a self-reliant, determined community of individuals intent on bettering their lives and those of their neighbors and friends.

1

THE FOUNDATIONS OF A COMMUNITY, 1673–1848

Our brethren from Fresh Meadows represented to the church that God has so blest and increased them of late.
—Reverend Isaac Backus of Middleborough, 1761

South Middleborough initially developed as the community of Fresh Meadows along the Weweantic River corridor where naturally occurring meadows attracted English settlement during the last quarter of the seventeenth and the first half of the eighteenth centuries. During these years, the foundations of South Middleborough as a Baptist community on the periphery of the older, more established Congregational presence at Middleborough center were established, a circumstance that would ultimately see South Middleborough evolve less rapidly than the town center. The first decades of South Middleborough's history also witnessed the development of a conservative religious, political and social ethic that distinguished the community from Middleborough center, which historically would be more diverse, more liberal, more permissive, more industrialized and more commercialized. While the locus of settlement at South Middleborough would ultimately shift by 1750 from Fresh Meadows to its present location near Wareham, Locust and Spruce Streets, the values of its earliest settlers would remain intact.

Topography and Early History

South Middleborough's present topography of swamps and flat, sandy terrain resulted from the final northward glacial recession when meltwater filled with sediment accumulated between two great glacial lobes creating what is known today as the Wareham outwash plain. The plain, a vast region of sandy soil extending through southern Plymouth County, is clearly identifiable today by its ground cover of white pine, pitch pine, scrub oak, huckleberry and other hardy plants capable of surviving in sandy soils and dry conditions. This circumstance would have later ramifications for South Middleborough, where the poverty of the soil would not prove conducive to extensive agriculture, and the crops that were eventually cultivated were those best suited to the soil of the region: hay, cranberries and white pine trees.

Despite the presence of the Weweantic River (known to the earliest settlers as the South Meadow River), the area of South Middleborough is not well drained. The river, formed by the union of Rocky Meadow and South Meadow Brooks, empties some fifty-five thousand acres before flowing into Buzzard's Bay. Just under twenty miles long, the river is notoriously winding. Its native name, in fact, means "wandering" in Wampanoag. Given South Middleborough's flat topography and poor drainage, swamps are prevalent.

Because of the relatively inhospitable nature of South Middleborough, the absence of large bodies of water and the poverty of the soil, South Middleborough appears to have been largely unsettled prior to 1690, though little is presently known of its native history. At the time the Europeans first became aware of the region, it was covered with heavy woodlands, interrupted occasionally by fresh meadows. The earliest records of the area are the South Purchase Proprietors' records, which date from the last decade of the seventeenth century. These records indicate the abundance of a variety of trees, including red, white and black oak, maple, poplar, pine, spruce and, to a lesser degree, cedar, "swamp" birch and willow. Also noted was "saxefax" (sassafras), growing well enough to have been considered a tree, and beech. Such trees undoubtedly had reached a formidable size, and at least two of the spruce trees recorded as boundary markers in the purchase were termed "great," an indication of the towering height and substantial girth of many trees in the district.

Undoubtedly, the vegetative growth at the time was heavy, as it remains in many areas today. South Middleborough is well known for the near

Illustrative of the profuse vegetation and swampy terrain that historically have covered much of South Middleborough is this photograph of a young Dorothy Wilber entitled "Dorothy May Stirs the Water" taken on March 24, 1935. The dense, brush-covered wetland hints at the topography encountered by the region's earliest English settlers, as well as the appeal of naturally occurring fresh meadows along the Weweantic River. *Courtesy of Middleborough Historical Association.*

impenetrability of its woods and swamps. During the 1959 national manhunt for William and John Coyle, the South Middleborough woods were described as "almost impassable," with "heavy underbrush and hip-deep swamps." Another indication of just how thick the South Middleborough undergrowth can be is the number of people over the years who have become lost in the woods there for extended periods of time. Even today, certain areas are marked on contemporary assessors' maps of Middleborough as "ground obscured dense trees."

The wooded and swampy landscape, however, was interrupted by fresh meadows, naturally occurring open spaces in the otherwise thick forest, particularly in the vicinity of the Weweantic River. It was the presence of these fresh meadows, coveted for their productivity, that initially attracted settlement. Henry Griffith, in his *History of the Town of Carver*, wrote that "the marsh meadows [on either side of the Weweantic] were the chief attraction" of the area. Known to be rich in soil, they were ready-made homesteads requiring no toilsome clearing, and their presence southwest of the small Plymouth settlement soon became known to the English, particularly the expansive South Meadows on the east bank of the Weweantic in present-day

Carver. Fresh meadows were also located in the area of South Middleborough along the west bank of the Weweantic River, north of present-day Pine Street. Because of the immense value of these meadows, when Plymouth's western boundary was established, it was set deliberately far enough inland "to include the south meadows…lately discovered, and the convenient Uplands there-abouts." Though South Middleborough, too, included fresh meadows along the bank of the Weweantic River, these presumably were not as extensive as those in Carver and were not well known. Nonetheless, they were expansive enough for the area to become known as Fresh Meadows (a name it would retain through the mid-nineteenth century) and to invite the first settlement in southern Middleborough.

The South and Snipatuit Purchases

Though Middleborough was formally incorporated as a town in 1669, only the northeastern quarter of the town as we know it today had been "purchased" from the natives and subsequently settled. The largest purchases—the South and the Sixteen Shilling—had yet to be made. This left two-thirds of the incorporated town (including South Middleborough) unpurchased and, consequently, unsettled. In order to open the enormous territory of South Middleborough to settlement and to exploit its resources, Benjamin Church of Duxbury and John Tomson of Barnstable, on behalf of the inhabitants of Middleborough, purchased from Tispaquin, the local Wampanoag sachem, and his son the southeastern portion of the town for just fifteen pounds on July 23, 1673. One-third of the tract (later known as the Snipatuit Purchase) would be reserved to Church and Tomson as payment for their services.

Settlement of the South Purchase, however, would have to wait until the conclusion of King Philip's War (1675–76), a conflict that otherwise had little impact on the area that would later become South Middleborough. The war, however, may have delayed development at South Middleborough as colonists returning to the town focused on rebuilding farmsteads destroyed in 1675. Little thought was given, and few resources were available, to open new settlement tracts like the South Purchase in the immediate aftermath of the war. Not until 1690 did the South Purchase Proprietors name John Soule, Isaac Howland and Jacob Tomson to lay out the purchase into lots,

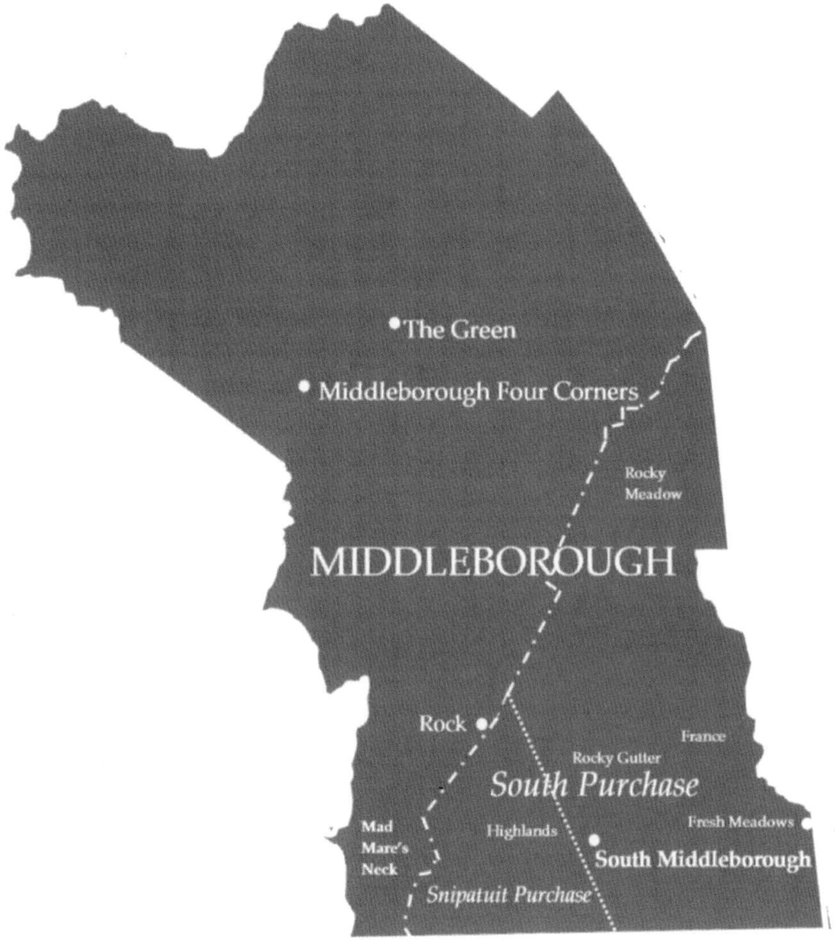

The South Purchase of 1673 was one of the largest land purchases at Middleborough. Not until the 1690s, however, would the purchase be divided into lots and thereby made available for settlement. The first settlers were attracted to naturally occurring meadows along the Weweantic River that gave their name to the settlement: Fresh Meadows. During the mid-eighteenth century, the locus of settlement shifted westward to the present "center" of South Middleborough.

agreeing that each proprietor should receive two. The three men divided the purchase into fifty-acre lots, over two hundred in all, and "couple[d] them as to make the shares as equal as [they] could."

South Middleborough appears to have been settled immediately following the assignment of the first South Purchase lots in the 1690s. As elsewhere, the settlement pattern was determined by a number of factors, including land quality and the proximity to routes of communication, and settlement at South Middleborough occurred initially along the Weweantic River corridor in proximity to the previously mentioned fresh meadows that would give the area its original name. The Fresh Meadows location also had the advantage of being located on the principal travel route between Plymouth and Rochester, which passed through the area and is today East and Beach Streets. Like the Nemasket River at Middleborough, the Weweantic River just downstream from the East Street Bridge appears to have had a wading place where the river was shallow enough to cross on foot. As early as the mid-1690s, a bridge appears to have been erected over the wading place, and it became known as Benson's Bridge due to the large number of that

Typical of the earliest houses built at South Middleborough was Hell's Blazes on Wareham Street, captured here in a photograph from 1934. Built in 1690, the house stood on eighty acres that occupied parts of the sixtieth and sixty-first South Purchase lots and was situated on the route linking Fresh Meadows and Plymouth with Dartmouth. *Courtesy of Library of Congress, Prints and Photographs Division, Historic American Buildings Survey, HABS MASS.12-MIDBO.5-1.*

family who inhabited the neighborhood at that time. Later, the bridge was moved upstream to its present site, where it remained known as the Fresh Meadows Bridge well into the nineteenth century.

It is believed that the house that was the original Hell's Blazes Tavern was built at this time, and if so, it was undoubtedly one of the earliest houses erected in the South Purchase. Although the main chimney of the original house had the date 1763 incised into one of the bricks, there were "indications that part of the house may have been built at an earlier date, possibly before 1700." In 1968, archaeological investigations by two members of the Plimouth Plantation Research Department seeking the foundations of older buildings on the property unearthed eighteenth-century pottery, clay pipe stems and other artifacts "consistent with the 1690 date."

The Economic Development of Fresh Meadows and a New Village

Fresh Meadows developed as the earliest settlement in southern Middleborough, with homes on either side of the Weweantic River, both in Middleborough and what is now Carver. While mid-sized farms devoted to agriculture remained the principal economic unit at Fresh Meadows throughout the eighteenth century, the Weweantic River at East Street emerged as an industrial site in the early 1700s, having first been developed with a sawmill and forge and later with mills, including a gristmill and combined board, shingle and stave mill, as well as a blacksmith shop. Certainly by 1734, a sawmill was operating there, taking advantage of the vast acreage of surrounding woodlands, and between 1734 and 1736, a forge seems to have been erected (in all likelihood) on the Carver side of the river.

Colonial iron making was a noted early industrial activity throughout the region due to the fortuitous presence of both iron ore and timber that could be used for fuel. Ore for Fresh Meadows was probably drawn locally from the swamps of the South Purchase, and one local lot there was, in fact, known as the "Ore Bed Lot," indicating that it was used as a source of iron for the local forges. Land was acquired on the north bank of the river in what is now Carver, and a dwelling house was erected there sometime between May 1734 and March 1736 "for the use of the Iron Works," indicating that the forge was then in operation. Also affiliated with the operation was a coal house that was raised sometime about 1742, at which time it was recorded as not having been completely shingled.

As late as 1842, East and Beach Streets remained the principal artery between Plymouth and New Bedford despite their likely poor condition (in 1937, East Street was characterized as "narrow, crooked and inconvenient for use and in need of specific repair, locating anew, or relocation"). Consequently, a number of taverns developed along the road at Fresh Meadows. As early as 1762, Joshua Benson is recorded as an "Inn Holder," and he was undoubtedly operating an inn in the Fresh Meadows neighborhood for travelers along the stage road from Plymouth to New Bedford. Most interesting of these inns was the Hole in the Wall, located at the intersection of East and Pine Streets just across from the Fresh Meadows industrial works. The house, in the early 1800s, was owned by Nathaniel Shurtleff Jr., who operated the curiously named inn. Writing in 1931, William B. Murdock explained how the name came about: "The hole in the wall was level with the floor in one room and level with the table top in another room and when thirsty stagecoach passengers sat about the table to rest and refresh themselves they would behold a jug of their hearts delight slide through the hole in the wall and out upon the table." The tavern was undoubtedly popular with workers at the nearby forge and was also used as a location for stabling horses by the Plymouth and New Bedford stage line, whose coaches passed along East Street, undoubtedly bringing with them much local news.

Farther south along East Street, at its intersection with Beach Street, was the neighborhood known as Bull Jump, allegedly named for the loud croaking of bullfrogs in the neighborhood, a somewhat unsettling sound on quiet spring evenings. Here was also located a tavern for travelers, though the date of its original establishment is unknown. Certainly, it was still in operation in the mid-1800s, conducted as a hotel by John Carver. Most famous of the taverns, however, was Hell's Blazes, then also on the main Plymouth–New Bedford route. Named "in all probability because it was frequented by workers from the smelting furnaces at what is now Tremont and nearby Carver," Hell's Blazes was later patronized by Daniel Webster in his travels between Marshfield and Cape Cod.

Despite the growth of Fresh Meadows, the locus of a new village settlement would be established in the mid-eighteenth century a few miles westward, where Consider Benson had cobbled a number of South Purchase lots into a 175-acre farm stretching from near the present junction of Spruce and

Throughout the eighteenth century, East and Beach Streets composed part of the main route between Plymouth and Dartmouth and became a natural site for taverns catering to travelers. Among them was the Hole in the Wall Tavern at the junction of East and Pine Streets at Fresh Meadows. By 1900, when it was photographed long after its heyday, the Hole in the Wall was a derelict structure.

Helping anchor the new location of South Middleborough was the South Middleborough Cemetery, seen in a photograph taken in the rear of the South Middleborough church on December 16, 1935. As was typical of many early burying grounds, by the 1890s, the South Middleborough Cemetery had become overgrown. Volunteers cleared grass and briars, and a cemetery association was established to oversee its maintenance. *Courtesy of Middleborough Historical Association.*

Locust Streets southeastward to Pine Street. On this farm, Benson built himself a home.

Others began erecting houses in the vicinity of what would become modern South Middleborough as well, including Thomas Raymond and his son Amos. By 1760, Amos Raymond had erected a house that stood in the neighborhood of the present South Middleborough church. The Smith-LeBaron-Hunt House on Locust Street is believed to have been built as early as 1750, as was the Simeon D. Wilbur House farther north on Wareham Street. The building on Spruce Street later known as the Mansion House probably dated from this time as well. Helping to solidify this area as the new "center" of South Middleborough was the location of the area's first formal burying ground, the South Middleborough Cemetery, which was established in 1768 on land given by Consider Benson and others, with its earliest burial occurring in 1771.

Third Calvinistic Baptist Church

Fresh Meadows and the newly emerging center of South Middleborough had become settled enough by the mid-eighteenth century to warrant the establishment of their own church. Previously, inhabitants of the area had been required to make the trek to the Green to attend Congregational services, a toilsome journey of several miles over what were undoubtedly poor roads.

As early as 1742, there is mention of a religious revival at Fresh Meadows, and by 1754, the Reverend Isaac Backus of the First Baptist Church of Middleborough was preaching in the neighborhood, which he clearly saw as fertile ground for his work. Backus recorded in his diary for July 17–18, 1755: "I went to Fresh Meadows and preacht at Mr. Caleb Bensons in the afternoon and my Soul had such bowels given me in pleading with sinners as I haven't had before a long time. And som souls were much moved upon. A time much to be remembered."

The growth of the Fresh Meadow Baptist group was significant enough to warrant the establishment of a formal church there in 1761, and Benson, William Parker, Caleb Cushman, Noah Benson, Francis Atwood and Deborah Benson requested to be dismissed from the First Baptist Church for this purpose. The dismissal was granted, and the small group set about

Though tempered by the popular colonial revival movement of the late nineteenth and early twentieth centuries, this 1934 photograph of a room in Hell's Blazes depicts the pared-down simplicity of the homes of early South Middleborough and is indicative of the relatively Spartan lives of the first settlers at Fresh Meadows. *Courtesy of Library of Congress, Prints and Photographs Division, Historic American Buildings Survey, HABS MASS.12-MIDBO.5-5.*

organizing the Third Baptist Church of Middleborough, which was formally established as a poll parish on August 4, 1761, with ten members. On that same day, the members signed seventeen articles of faith, and it is from this act that the history of organized religion is dated in South Middleborough. The first order of business for the new Third Church was to seek a pastor to settle in the community. On October 4, 1761, the Baptists at Fresh Meadows were able to inform the First Church "that God has displayed his grace among them considerably of late, and has united their hearts in the choice of Mr. Ebenezer Jones for their pastor." The selection of Jones was to prove a fateful choice.

THE CONTENTIOUS MINISTRY OF REVEREND EBENEZER JONES (1763–1771)

The man selected by the Third Baptist Church of Middleborough as its first pastor was Reverend Ebenezer Jones of Norton, Massachusetts, who is believed to have preached at Fresh Meadows prior to his ordination. Contrary to assertions that the South Middleborough church "thrived under the dynamic leadership of Rev. Ebenezer Jones," Jones's leadership would prove divisive, and the church would flourish despite, rather than because of, this. In fact, Matthew H. Cushing would later describe the years of Jones's pastorate as a "furnace of affliction."

Having been called to fill the pulpit at South Middleborough, Jones was ordained on October 28, 1761, with the assistance of Elder Isaac Backus and Deacon Shaw of the First Baptist Church of Middleborough. Jones's ordination was followed in the spring of 1762 by a religious revival at South Middleborough, "which prevailed through the year and spread into many other societies; the good fruits whereof were long visible." Though members were attracted from the neighboring areas of Carver, Wareham and Rochester, which were without Baptist parishes of their own, such good news was not long-lived, and the small Third Baptist congregation was soon riven with controversy in the second year of Jones's pastorate.

The conflict that would ultimately lead to several years of turmoil for the young church was based in a temporal rather than spiritual dispute, Reverend Jones having felt shortchanged by his new congregation in the matter of a house lot, which the congregation had agreed to provide him. Additionally, Jones may have been motivated by a desire to subvert the influence of Deacon Caleb Benson, the acknowledged lay leader of the congregation who himself may have felt threatened by the new pastor. At a March 11, 1763 meeting of the church, Jones gave voice to his frustration, complaining "of [Deacon Caleb Benson] beyond what was reasonable about Ch.'s not getting land for him…as he had encouraged him they would." Jones's speech at the meeting "implied a charge of wrong" upon Benson, which, because of the esteem in which Benson was held by the community, "inflamed" the congregation. On March 24, Backus was called to mediate the matter, the usual practice of religious societies at that time. Jones admitted to Backus that he had been intemperate in his language and confessed "that he was wrong in delivering out such a speech before the society, before matters had been laboured upon in church, tho' he still thought the deacon to be faulty."

Subsequent efforts to moderate the conflict were unsuccessful. Several members of the congregation, offended by Jones's comments regarding Benson, remained recalcitrant and refused to accept a repentant Jones as their pastor. Later, Backus privately confided his personal belief that Jones's wife was largely responsible for the slander against Benson. In his history, Backus attributes virtually the entire controversy to Mrs. Jones, remarking that "some evil behavior in Mr. Jones's wife, which drew him into a snare, caused a great division in the church and society." Nonetheless, Benson, too, came in for his share of criticism from Backus, especially for his ongoing efforts "to cast off [rather] than to reclaim the elder."

One tale told of Hell's Blazes' taproom (seen here in 1934) was that the Middleborough-Rochester town line passed through the building, and patrons would move to the opposite end of the room to circumvent anti-liquor laws in either community. Though untrue, the tale indicates the growing temperance influence of the Baptist and Methodist churches. *Courtesy of Library of Congress, Prints and Photographs Division, Historic American Buildings Survey, HABS MASS.12-MIDBO.5-6.*

For two years, a portion of the congregation remained intransigent, refusing to either restore Jones to his pastorate or grant the recommendation the pastor requested in return for agreeing to be dismissed. In addition to deeply dividing the community, the ongoing stalemate had unforeseen financial consequences for all parishioners. To avoid payment of taxes that were levied in each community for the support of the standing Congregational Church, members of other denominations were required to present tax exemption certificates signed by the pastors of their churches. Because the congregation refused to reinstate Jones as pastor, there was no one to sign tax exemption certificates for Third Church members, and the Town of Middleborough accordingly proceeded to levy church taxes upon the South Middleborough Baptists. "The Baptists claimed that this was sheer malevolence, since the parish knew very well that they were bona fide Baptists. But the assessors had the letter of the law on their side, and the courts upheld them." From that day forward, local taxation would remain a concern of South Middleborough residents.

Despite the hostility of a large part of his congregation, Reverend Jones remained at Fresh Meadows to minister informally to those who continued to follow his lead throughout 1764 and 1765, during which time the church members were meeting at Elijah Williams's house. Such a situation, however, could not continue indefinitely. On October 15, 1765, a council of the First and Second Middleborough Baptist Churches, along with the church from Norton, once more met at Fresh Meadows to revisit the controversy. After hearing members of the Third Church, the council concluded that "the major part of the church were united with Elder Jones to go on in the worship of God together," but it declined to take action against the church members who "still stand off," despite their blatant refusal to reinstate Jones. Because the council would not compel the church to reinstate Jones as pastor, it had to call for Jones "to refrain from administering special ordinances." Jones had no alternative but to leave the South Middleborough church without a recommendation, and his main accomplishment in enlarging the congregation, despite the rancor, went unrecognized. During his pastorate, about fifty new members had been added to the church.

Ministry of Reverend Asa Hunt (1771–1789)

Reverend Ebenezer Jones was succeeded in 1771 by Reverend Asa Hunt. Hunt was born at Braintree and had preached for a time in the Baptist church at Raynham. He was ordained pastor of the Third Baptist Church of Middleborough at Fresh Meadows on October 30, 1771, with an ordination sermon by Isaac Backus, who took as his text II Corinthians 3:6 ("Who also hath made us able ministers of the new testament; not of the letter, but of the spirit; for the letter killeth, but the spirit giveth life").

Backus describes Hunt's preaching as "acceptable," an important consideration given the divisive history of the church prior to Hunt's arrival. Hunt's tenure as South Middleborough's pastor was noteworthy for a number of reasons, not the least of which was the healing he brought to a discordant congregation.

Constructed about 1773 as a consequence of an ecclesiastical conflict within the church, the original South Middleborough parsonage on Spruce Street served until 1867. At the time that Reverend E.W. Barrows was residing here during the late 1850s, the property was described as "a ministerial farm of 50 acres furnishing a quiet home and an abundance of wood for the pastor's family." *Photograph by Michael J. Maddigan.*

Following the community's rancorous relationship with Reverend Jones, which had been triggered by the inadequacy of the community's financial support for the ministry, efforts were undertaken to obviate this as a future source of conflict with the creation of a ministerial lot, a lot of land that would be devoted exclusively to the support of the local Baptist ministry. In 1773, a group of forty-six individuals from Middleborough, Carver, Rochester and Wareham contributed to the purchase of a lot of land on Spruce Street upon which a small parsonage was constructed. Succeeding pastors were offered the use of the lot and parsonage, as noted by Isaac Backus, who recorded that the Third Church had furnished Jones's successor with not only "a good place for a settlement" but also "the use of the ministerial lot."

Hunt assumed the pastorate of the South Middleborough church during a politically volatile time in the nation, and although South Middleborough

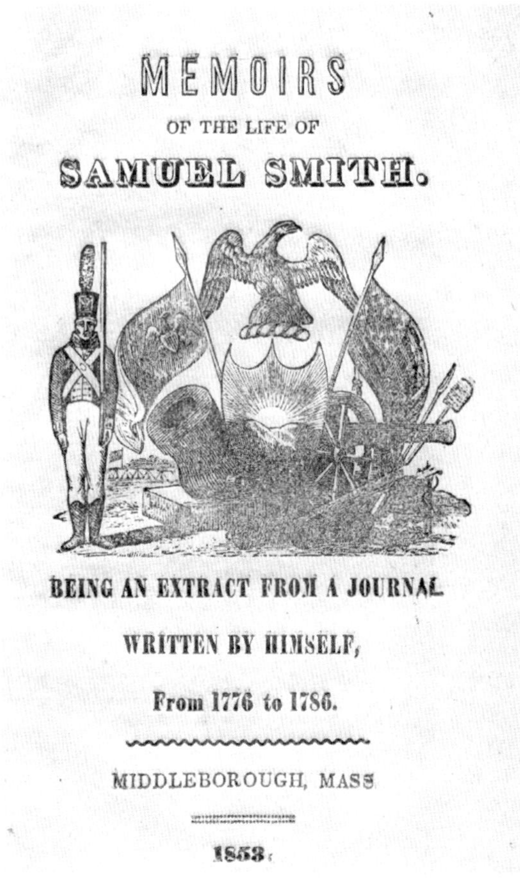

Samuel Smith's avowed purpose in recording his Revolutionary War recollections as a member of the Rhode Island regiment was to inform his friends of his earlier trials nearly three-quarters of a century earlier and to provide a small token to those who might give him financial assistance in his old age. It remains one of the few surviving firsthand accounts of the war. *Courtesy of Middleborough Historical Association.*

seemed largely immune from the political rhetoric that flowed elsewhere in Middleborough, a number of South Middleborough residents would serve in the Revolutionary War. Lieutenant Josiah Smith, who has been identified as living both in South Middleborough and in France (the area just north of Fresh Meadows along present-day France Street), is stated to have been only the second man to enter Fort Ticonderoga following its capture by Ethan Allen. Samuel Smith, who later settled in South Middleborough, enjoyed a remarkably varied Revolutionary experience, witnessing the execution of Major André; fighting in the struggle against the Hessians, "which marked the turning point of the war"; and enduring the dreadful winter of 1777–78 at Valley Forge. Later, in 1853, Smith would publish his *Memoirs of Samuel Smith: A Soldier of the Revolution (1776–1786)* recounting his wartime experiences, and his small pamphlet is one of the few firsthand accounts of the Revolutionary War extant today. The notorious Deborah Sampson, who disguised herself as a man in order to fight in the war, had South Middleborough connections as well. In 1782, Sampson was reprimanded by the Third Baptist Church of Middleborough for "dressing in a man's clothing and enlisting as a soldier in the army." She was also charged with being "very loose and un-Christian like." Today, she is considered an American heroine.

The Spruce Meetinghouse Prompts New Growth

Significantly, it was during Hunt's pastorate that a meetinghouse was finally raised in 1774 for the church that had been without one since its establishment in 1761. The meetinghouse was built immediately to the west of the South Middleborough Cemetery and was a large two-story structure that was unpainted and unheated. It became known as the Spruce Meetinghouse. According to Jennie Gammons, "The origin of the name may have come from the fact that spruce shingles covered the building from top to bottom, unpainted without and within. A spruce tree may have been the central figure."

The location of the new meetinghouse (and nearby South Middleborough's first school) also helped entrench the vicinity as the new "center" of South Middleborough, in contrast to Fresh Meadows, which was increasingly being abandoned. In fact, the new neighborhood took its earliest name from the church and was known as Spruce until Stillman Benson suggested the less evocative name of South Middleborough in the 1840s. The development of a new village center attracted residents anxious to be near both church and school. A number of houses were constructed in the vicinity of the church during this period, including the Thomas House (1776) on Wareham Street near Spruce Street and the Smith-Wallen-Ryder House (circa 1803) at 36 Spruce Street. Most unusual of all, however, was the so-called Stone House (1828), which was raised directly to the east of the cemetery. Romaine's *History of the Town of Middleboro* recounts that the middle portion of the house was reportedly built by a "Mr. Manning, a man of Dutch descent" who "disappeared from the community" shortly thereafter. Lorenzo Sturtevant added the wings on either side of Manning's house but apparently ran out of funds, as they were left roofless. Stillman Benson completed the house, coating the stone walls with white plaster and adding a decorative red bargeboard along the eaves. The first family to actually reside in the house was that of Calvin M. Gammons later in the century.

The so-called Stone House on Wareham Street, which takes its name from the material used in its construction, was one of the most unusual structures ever built at South Middleborough. Erected during the post-Revolutionary expansion of South Middleborough, its first occupant was Calvin Gammons and his family. It was subsequently owned by two more generations of the Gammons family, who used it for rental purposes. *Courtesy of Middleborough Historical Association.*

Post-Revolutionary Change

The post-Revolutionary period in South Middleborough was a period of not only tremendous political and physical changes in the village but also equally significant social change, particularly within the church, which was the beneficiary of a tremendous religious revival following 1780. The ubiquitous Isaac Backus recorded that "such a work of the Spirit of God began among them in March, 1780, as caused the addition of one hundred and thirteen members to their church by September, 1782, when they had one hundred and ninety-four in all." Hunt would eventually see some 140 new members added to the church during the course of his ministry. Baptisms were performed in a number of locations throughout the area, including the Weweantic River, Bates Pond in nearby Carver, a small pond on the farm of Ezra Maxim and a pool on the Thomas Farm on Wareham Street that was created by damming a small brook.

Two developments, however, threatened the expansion of the congregation. First, Reverend Hunt's personal finances became a matter of public concern when Hunt became financially overextended and could not honor his debts. Hunt, embarrassed by his circumstances, requested to be dismissed from the church, and this request was granted with reluctance in December 1789.

Second, there was mounting dissension among the congregation concerning the removal of some members to Beaver Dam (later known as Rock) a couple miles to the northwest. Reverend Hunt's dismissal had left the Third Church without a settled pastor for a number of years, and in May 1793, ten church members living in Rock engaged Reverend Samuel Nelson (1745–1822) to preach there. Additionally, the establishment of North Rochester as a separate parish further deprived the South Middleborough church of members, and not all those who remained were committed to the seriousness of Sunday worship. Backus recorded, "The church was in low circumstances, and young people got to be so extravagant in vanity that they could hardly be kept civil in times of public worship." Such attitudes, unthinkable prior to the war, were gradually becoming the norm. Earlier, the Third Church had been required to discipline Deborah Sampson for disguising herself as a male soldier. Now, once more, the youth of the community were seen as acting with little regard for either religious or social propriety. Within a month of Nelson's settlement as pastor, however, the situation speedily improved.

Backus noted that at the start of June 1793, the "old Christians became all alive in religion." Meetings were heavily attended "without the least disturbance from vain persons, which before were so troublesome." To the moderating influence of Reverend Nelson was this change undoubtedly attributed, thereby enhancing the influence of the Rock faction that had initially engaged him. In 1795, their goal was finally accomplished when a new Baptist meetinghouse was constructed in Rock, effectively sealing the fate of South Middleborough.

Without a church of their own, the remaining members in South Middleborough were eventually attracted to the church at Carver, "where there was much sectarian activity in the early 1800s" and the two groups established the Baptist Church of Carver and Middleboro. This church grew to be so large in numbers that the South Middleborough Baptists were advised to form their own church, but they never did so. Instead, the Baptists' place was taken by the Reformed Methodists, who, like Backus's congregation, were noted for their evangelism and consequently attracted many converts from among the inhabitants of South Middleborough.

The Cape-style Simeon D. Wilbur House on Wareham Street was indicative of the appearance of South Middleborough homes prior to the advent of the nineteenth century. Occupied by Jesse Vaughan in 1855 and later by the family of Simeon D. Wilbur, in the early 1800s the house commanded an extensive farm. It was so badly gutted by fire in 2009 that it was demolished. *Courtesy of Middleborough Historical Association.*

Economically, South Middleborough's Federal era was dominated by large, single-family subsistence farms belonging to the Thomas and Smith families, Stillman Benson, Jairus Gammons, Daniel Doten and others. These farms occupied extensive tracts of land, including agricultural and forested land, and crops probably consisted mostly of rye and corn. While industrial works continued to operate at Fresh Meadows, the removal of the principal settlement from there to South Middleborough hampered the area's economic development as the sole source of power remained the Weweantic River, and South Middleborough's economic growth would be held in check until steam technology in the mid-nineteenth century freed the community from reliance on water power. Without much industry, South Middleborough was likely little affected by the War of 1812 or the Jeffersonian embargo that so hampered business development elsewhere, including Middleborough center.

Social life remained dominated by the overlapping and pervasive influence of the old Baptist and new Methodist churches. The growing influence of Reformed Methodism tended to promote opposition to slavery and adherence to temperance, two important reform movements that would occupy much of the church's attention throughout the nineteenth century. South Middleborough, on the eve of the railroad's arrival, remained a socially conservative, religiously evangelical, agricultural community.

2

AN AGRICULTURAL ECONOMY EMERGES, 1848–1872

A railroad coming down from Boston entered the…region and changed the morals, manners, and occupations of its inhabitants.
—William Root Bliss, Colonial Times on Buzzards Bay *(1901)*

The course of South Middleborough would be irrevocably altered with the 1848 arrival of the Cape Cod Branch Railroad, the impact of which was revolutionary. In 1901, local colorist William Root Bliss noted the economic and social implications of the Cape Cod Railroad's arrival in neighboring West Wareham when he reflected on the vast changes its arrival wrought. Truly, the railroad brought with it both economic and social change to all the villages through which it passed.

The establishment of a railroad station at present-day South Middleborough, and with it a post office, would help entrench the village as a small regional center at the expense of the older locus at Fresh Meadows. The general availability of rail transport following 1848 ensured that South Middleborough's staple products found their way to a ready market throughout the northeastern United States, thereby fostering the development of a commercial agricultural economy dominated by the production of lumber, as well as hay, cranberries, ice and charcoal, and encouraging the growth of ancillary industries, including trunk, box, cranberry implement and soap manufacturing, albeit on a smaller scale.

CAPE COD BRANCH RAILROAD

Incorporated in April 1846, the Cape Cod Branch Railroad Company was empowered by the Massachusetts General Court to construct a single-track railroad from the existing Fall River Railroad line near that company's depot at Middleborough center southeastward through Middleborough, Rochester and Wareham to Sandwich on Cape Cod. While the route selected passed through the heart of South Middleborough, it is somewhat unclear whether a station would have been established there had it not been for the influence of Stillman Benson, a man "whose name stood for high finance in the community." As early as January 1835, Benson was characterized as "a young man of intelligence and honest report," and in 1838 he was elected to the state legislature. Though Benson served only one term as a state representative, he continued to hold office locally as a Middleborough selectman (1839–46 and 1872–73). In 1843, he was appointed a justice of the peace, being "engaged extensively in the settlement of estates, serving as administrator, executor, guardian and commissioner" and wielding much influence in the South Middleborough community.

Benson may have purchased stock in the Cape Cod Branch Railroad at the time of its incorporation; certainly at the time of his death, he owned shares in the Old Colony Railroad, the successor firm of the Cape Cod Branch. Also, in 1846 Benson may have been contemplating the establishment of a sawmill, and the prospect of securing a likely heavy user of its proposed freight services may have served as further inducement for the railroad to locate a station at South Middleborough.

Not all were enthused about the prospect of the railroad. A tale told by one later South Middleborough chronicler reveals that Samuel Smith, the Revolutionary War Patriot, was vehemently opposed to the location of the railroad's right of way through Smith family property:

> *His contentment was disturbed when his estate was divided by the railroad…Mr. Smith who had endured all sorts of hardships, even the frozen Winter at Valley Forge, was ready to fight an iron monster when it desecrated his land. So he stood on the track at the approach of the engine with its rumbling train. He took no heed of the warning whistle as it screamed in his ears. Nearer and nearer, around the curve in full sight came the giant, puffing its black smoke, but the old soldier did not budge. The*

engineer sighted the figure and in fright slowed down. "Get off," he shouted, "or I'll run over you," as his hand moved to the throttle, the old man knew he was beaten and sullenly moved away. For a long time, he cherished a grudge, but became pacified when he realized the advantage the railroad provided for the community.

A site for a station was selected on the east side of Spruce Street just south of its intersection with Wareham (now Locust) Street. The original depot consisted of a station, freight house and single track, and its presence in South Middleborough was pivotal in the community's economic development following the mid-nineteenth century, permitting the community to engage in the profitable exploitation of its timber and other agricultural resources. The station included a siding for freight cars, as well as for the convenience of the Sandwich trains that met the Boston trains at this point on the one-track line at four o'clock each afternoon during the early years of the railroad. (Sadly, this awkward arrangement whereby trains backed onto the siding in order to permit the down-Cape train to pass on the main track would result

The South Middleborough railroad station (seen here in the late 1800s with its 1878 depot) was established largely through the influence of Stillman Benson. The local railroad provided access to markets and permitted South Middleborough residents to profitably exploit local resources of standing white pine timber. White pine lumber, boxboards, trunks and cordwood all flowed in quantity through the station.

in the worst accident the South Middleborough station would ever witness when, in 1859, the Hyannis train collided head-on with the Boston train.)

The railroad (renamed the Cape Cod Railroad in 1854) appears to have been constructed by Irish labor throughout 1846 and 1847, and the progress of building was not without conflict. Deacon Alfred Wood of Middleborough recorded in his notes of Middleborough deaths that in July 1847, Patrick Lawrence was "murdered by Michael Donegan on R.R. in South Middleboro," an event about which little else is known.

The first fifteen miles of the road between Middleborough center and Wareham were opened to the public on January 26, 1848, with the remaining link between Wareham and Sandwich opening shortly thereafter. Initially, the railroad operated two passenger trains and one freight train daily, with the exception of Sundays.

Despite the fact that South Middleborough felt itself fairly well convenienced by the railroad's freight service, which during this period would transport South Middleborough products such as lumber, trunks, boxes and spools to a wider market, it was less enamored of the road's passenger service. "It costs sixty cents to ride fourteen miles from Wareham to Middleborough on the defuncted, fizzled-out Cape Cod railroad," sputtered the *Middleboro Gazette* in November 1872, just one month after the Cape Cod's consolidation with the Old Colony & Newport Railroad Company. The newspaper's comments would be the first of many over the course of the following sixty-plus years concerning South Middleborough residents' concerns with the viability and economy of transportation between Wareham and Middleborough.

THE FOUNDATION OF THE LUMBER INDUSTRY

The arrival of the railroad was responsible for stimulating the economies of the various local villages through which it passed. Certainly, the railroad's presence was indispensable to the ultimate development of South Middleborough's lumber industry following 1848, allowing the community to profitably exploit the timber resources that blanketed the area. While such stands of timber had always proven a valuable asset, never before had the residents had the means to transport the product of these forests to markets hungry for building and packing material. The Cape Cod Railroad would provide that means.

It was in South Middleborough that "the most extensive pine woods of the town" were located, stretching beyond the town limits into neighboring Carver and Rochester. The white pine was then more highly valued than it is today, and the sandy soil of the region ensured the trees' abundant propagation relative to moisture-loving hardwoods. Concerns that other communities might have had relative to overcutting forested lands seemed to apply little to South Middleborough's pine woods; "their rapid growth has been remarkable and they have not materially diminished, notwithstanding the large amount of timber used in the lumber mills," noted one local nineteenth-century lumberman. The rapidity of growth was a key factor in the industry's development, ensuring that local pines would grow to merchantable size quickly enough to preclude depletion of the local supply.

South Middleborough's forests fueled the production of wooden goods, including lumber, boxboards, slabs, cordwood, spools, trunks, boxes and box shooks, shipment of which to places as far distant as New York and Philadelphia was facilitated by the railroad. And though white pine, because of its recognition as a useful, all-purpose wood, was the basis for South Middleborough's prosperity, other woods were in demand—most notably birch, the supply of which went almost wholly into the local production of thread spools. Birch was noted for its resiliency to stains and therefore lent itself to spool manufacturing, having found favor among thread makers.

It is difficult to ascertain the extent of South Middleborough's forests in the early nineteenth century prior to the establishment of the local lumber industry due largely to a dearth of recorded evidence. Presumably, though, some of South Middleborough's pinelands had been created on worn-out or unproductive lands, and the incidences of local farmers setting pines out on such land elsewhere in Middleborough were recorded throughout the period. The reforesting of Middleborough's "waste lands," though uncoordinated and frequently motivated by curiosity rather than profit, was altering the physical landscape during these years, resulting in an increasingly forested community. One commentator, speaking in 1884, remarked that he had "ascertained by an examination that I made several years ago, that there were at that time about five thousand acres of woodland in the town of Middleborough more than there were fifty years previously."

Close by was the experience of Huckleberry Corner, just over the Middleborough town line in Carver. Fields on which, in 1806, "naught was seen but sand and large weeds" were by 1866 "covered with a thrifty growth

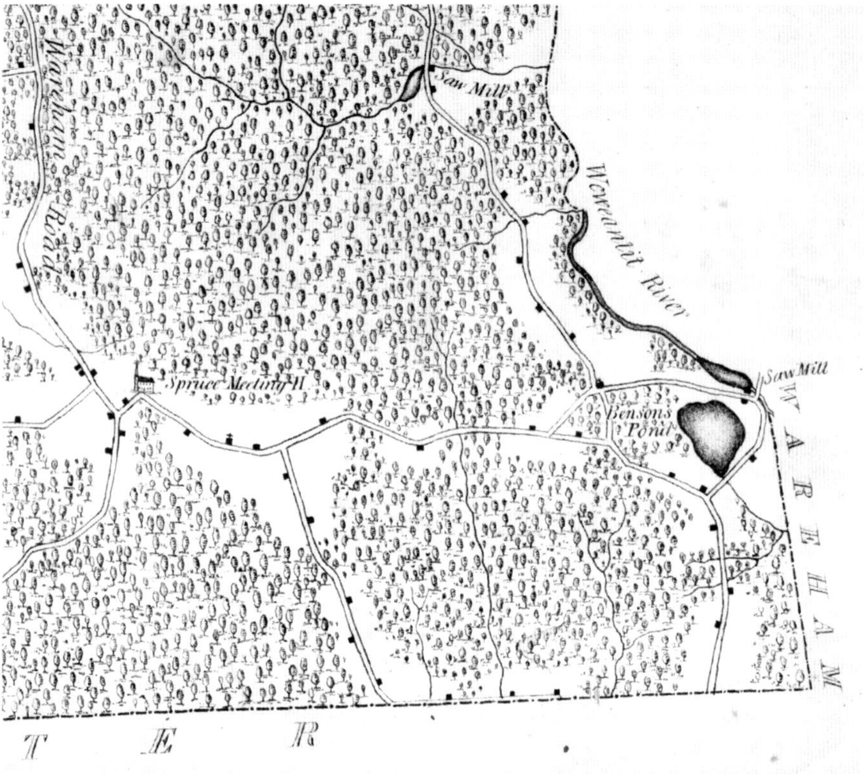

By the first decades of the 1800s, the South Middleborough economy was firmly rooted in subsistence agriculture. The arrival of the Cape Cod Branch Railroad in 1848, however, would permit the community to exploit the vast acreage of standing white pine timber that blanketed the area, a resource that is clearly shown on this detail of Samuel S. Bourne's 1831 map of Middleborough.

of wood." Differences in the 1831 and 1855 maps of Middleborough clearly demonstrate the reforestation of the Weweantic River corridor, where farmsteads were abandoned when the population locus shifted to South Middleborough in the mid-eighteenth century. This process of reforestation was also encouraged by the introduction of coal as a heating fuel, the disappearance of sheep and the decreasing size of cattle herds. The reforestation of South Middleborough, coupled with the establishment of the Cape Cod Branch Railroad with its station at South Middleborough, laid the foundation for the community's development as a lumbering center in the last half of the nineteenth century.

Industrial and Commercial Development

South Middleborough's sawmills would literally become the engines that would drive the community's economic growth during the latter half of the nineteenth century. The sawmill at Fresh Meadows standing on a dam across the Weweantic River between Middleborough and Carver was the oldest sawmill operating in South Middleborough and was still run by the power of the river. The introduction and application of steam power to industry, and specifically lumber milling, however, permitted business concerns to relocate anywhere they chose and to no longer be dependent on water sources like the Weweantic River.

Benson & Smith was likely the first steam-powered sawmill at South Middleborough, formed as a partnership between Revolutionary Patriot Samuel Smith's son, Chandler R. Smith, and Stillman Benson in the early 1850s. The sawmill was located at South Middleborough opposite the depot on the south side of the railroad track and engaged in the manufacture of pine boxes, though it also produced other goods. In September 1858, the firm was manufacturing one hundred dozen trunk bodies and four hundred gross spools per week, along with "innumerable" boxes for Seth Fowle & Company, a Boston-based medicine manufacturer, as well as valise woods, shingles, boards and other items. Twelve to fifteen men were employed there, and the mill was powered by a twenty-horsepower engine. The biggest demand was for pine for the production of shipping boxes and the manufacture of trunk bodies, though birch wood was also sought by the firm for the production of its spools.

The nearby intersection of Wareham (now Locust) and Spruce Streets, which was later known as Clark's Corner, emerged during this period as the center of South Middleborough, the railroad helping foster the development of commercial enterprise there. It was natural that the community would grow around the station, where retail goods could be received and manufactured goods shipped. Both A. Cobb and Chandler R. Smith conducted "West India Goods & Groceries" businesses near Clark's Corner. Still another store was said to have been started as a community effort to aid its pastor, Reverend Theophilus S. Brown, by providing him with a supplemental income. The tasks of pastor and shopkeeper proved too daunting to manage simultaneously, and the well-intentioned gesture proved "an unwise proceeding and no blessing to the pastor." At Clark's Corner, too, was South Middleborough's post office, established in 1846

Zalmon Tobey Wallen, the son-in-law of Chandler R. Smith, engaged in shoe manufacturing on a small scale at South Middleborough for a short period in the 1850s. Wallen later operated a billiard hall at Middleborough Center, an occupation that undoubtedly raised eyebrows among his more conservative South Middleborough neighbors. Wallen's son Frank L. Wallen was later station agent of the South Middleborough station. *Courtesy of Middleborough Historical Association.*

with the railroad's arrival. Cyrus LeBaron served as the community's first postmaster and was succeeded by Chandler R. Smith, Nathaniel Sears, Simeon D. Wilbur, John S. Benson and James M. Clark Jr. In 1855, the store and post office shared a home on the southeast corner of Locust and Spruce Streets. Proto-industrialization was noted, as well. In January 1858, Zalmon T. Wallen was listed among Middleborough boot and shoe manufacturers as operating in South Middleborough, an indication that the operation consisted of more than a mere cobbler's shop. By 1859, this operation was probably in the hands of Nathaniel Sears and was located near the depot.

THE FIRE OF MAY 27, 1859

The nascent economic growth of South Middleborough, however, would experience a severe setback when a devastating fire on May 27, 1859, destroyed several buildings in the heart of the village, removing with them the community's aspirations of developing an industrial base. Destroyed were the sawmill of Benson & Smith, the Cape Cod Railroad depot and the combined post office and shoe manufactory of Nathaniel Sears.

The fire broke out about ten o'clock in the evening in the Benson & Smith mill, presumably originating in an engine in the plant, but was not discovered until the mill was completely engulfed in flames. As reported by the *Namasket Gazette*, the entire mill was lost:

> *The flames spread very rapidly to the depot of the Cape Cod Railroad, burning on its way about twenty cords of wood belonging to the Railroad, Benson & Smith, Ansel Smith, and Whitcomb Ryder. All the books, tickets, etc., belonging to the Railroad, were burnt with the depot; also, twenty-five bus*[hels] *of corn and meal belonging to Mr. Taylor, North Rochester.*

Benson & Smith sustained the heaviest loss in the fire, about $5,000. Destroyed along with the mill was its engine, sewing machine, several saws, a planing and shingle machine, a matcher, spool machinery, several thousands of boards that were stored in the building and fourteen hundred gross of spools awaiting shipment. The firm was completely uninsured. Nathaniel Sears lost about $100 worth of shoemaking tools and two cases of completed ready-made shoes. Though the post office was leveled, "very little mail matter was lost." Chandler Smith's house opposite the depot briefly caught fire, and he lost two haystacks in the blaze. Additionally, "the iron rails on the track were heated red hot, and warped out of their fastenings towards the mill."

The May calamity helped check the industrialization of South Middleborough. The shoe manufactory never was rebuilt, and though the sawmill was, it was moved away from the depot, thereby ensuring the depot's future safety but also limiting the likelihood of an industrial base arising near it.

The community had barely begun to rebuild following the calamitous fire of May 1859, when on July 18 of that same year, it became the scene of a horrific railroad accident when the Hyannis and Boston trains collided head-on. Coming so soon after the South Middleborough fire, the train accident proved another debilitating blow, not only for South Middleborough, but also for the Cape Cod Railroad. Yet despite these accidents, and others, the Cape Cod was still able to make a reasonably good financial showing at the end of the year, a fact that the *Namasket Gazette* understandably found somewhat surprising. "The past has been a disastrous year, on account of casualties and accidents, and it is extremely fortunate that so good an exhibit of the company's affairs can be made."

THE INFLUENCE OF THE REFORMED METHODIST CHURCH

Undoubtedly helping the community weather the crisis in 1859 was its strong sense of sodality fostered by the local Reformed Methodist Society. In writing the history of this church for inclusion in his *History of the Town of Middleboro*, Thomas Weston remarked that "there is no continuing history of any religious organization [at South Middleborough] from 1795 to 1868." Ebenezer W. Peirce was equally frustrated in his attempts to document the South Middleborough church's history. "As this church has sometimes been of that branch called the 'Reformed' and sometimes of that denomination 'Episcopal,' the tracing of its minute history is rendered exceedingly difficult, and perhaps to a considerable degree impossible." (Matthew H. Cushing later attributed this lack of information to "a certain pastor who was clerk of the church, [who] carried away whatever records that had been made prior to 1840.")

The Reformed Methodist denomination was established in 1814 by Elder Pliny Brett, who felt the established Methodist Church to be in dire need of reformation. In 1825, a Reformed Methodist congregation was established at South Middleborough and began holding services in the abandoned Spruce Meetinghouse. An immediate religious revival took place in 1827, and early pastors at this time included Reverend Uriah Minor (1830–35), Reverend Lorenzo D. Johnson and his brother Thomas, Reverend Elijah Bailey and Theophilus Brown (1841–48).

During Brown's pastorate, the Spruce Meetinghouse (which was, in its final years, described as "weather-beaten and decadent" and "inadequate for the times") was razed in 1844, and the present church building was erected in its stead by Benjamin F. Harlow. A "daring sailor" was reportedly employed to climb to the top of the old church to perform "the most perilous tasks" of demolition, and much of the lumber from the demolished church was utilized in the construction of its replacement. Also under Brown, a church reorganization took place, though details are lacking.

Despite the absence of records between 1848 and 1868, the church appears to have been active. Both Parley Brown and Jacob Wallen are listed as Reformed Methodist ministers resident at South Middleborough in 1855, when they may have been serving as temporary pastors. (That same year, in May, the *Namasket Gazette* received a bottle from Reverend Wallen "of his great remedy for Catarrh.")

During the mid-1850s, yet another small revival occurred, with the local *Gazette* being "informed by Rev. Mr. Marks of So. Middleboro, that some 20 of his Congregation have recently indulged hopes and the interest still continues." The congregation may have had difficulties attracting Reformed Methodists as preachers, for Marks was succeeded in the 1850s by "a clergyman of the Christian Baptist denomination," Reverend E.W. Barrows, who was nonetheless "held in high esteem by the people, as a worthy, efficient, and sound teacher of Christianity." Under Barrows's influence, a revival was evident in September 1858, and it was recorded that "prosperity and peace attend the society at the S[outh] M[iddleborough] Chapel." At the time, the church had some forty-five members and a congregation numbering between 150 and 200. Additionally, there was a large choir "that sing[s] with such spirit," a Sunday school and an "efficient" Ladies' Sewing Circle.

During Barrows's pastorate, the First Reformed Methodist Society and the Protestant Methodist Church merged in 1858 to form the Reformed Methodist Church. Ten years later, in 1868, under the direction of pastor John G. Gammons, the church was once again reorganized, this time as a Methodist Episcopal Church, thereby severing its affiliation with the Reformed Methodists, a denomination that had been on the decline since the 1840s.

Evidencing the strength of the local congregation at this time was the 1874–75 reconstruction of the church, during which the chapel was raised, an additional ten feet to house a kitchen constructed onto the north end and seven feet for a vestibule and two stairways added to the south end. Additionally, a vestry was built beneath the enlarged building. According to one South Middleborough resident of the time, "The young men of the community joined in digging the excavation for the vestry, and in raising funds [by sponsoring a play and a Fourth of July picnic], believing that the reward for their efforts would be use of the building for their 'sociables.' They were told, after the work was completed, that this was to be a place of worship and not a social center." At the time, the vestry was equipped with settees at a cost of $41, the same settees selling seventy-five years later for more than $300 in May 1950, when they were replaced with folding chairs. The completed church was reopened on Saturday, February 6, 1875, with a sermon by S.F. Upham, DD.

The church finally assumed its modern appearance when in 1879 the belfry was added and a bell installed during the pastorate of Reverend Isaac

The South Middleborough Methodist Church was constructed as a one-story chapel building on the site of the earlier Spruce Meetinghouse in 1844. The building was enlarged and altered over the course of several years in the late nineteenth century to assume its present appearance. This view dates from the late 1800s. *Courtesy of Middleborough Historical Association.*

Sherman. As later recalled by Jennie Gammons, the bell called worshippers to prayer throughout the week and "tolled solemnly for funeral processions, its jangling tones hurriedly announced a forest fire and prankish tones at midnight welcomed the glorious 4th of July."

During the mid- and late nineteenth century, the church remained a strong arbiter of the community's religious and social life. Temperance, in particular, was a strongly held value at South Middleborough and one with severe legal repercussions for transgressors of the law. Yet another area in which the South Middleborough church undoubtedly influenced the social consciousness of the community was in regard to slavery. While there is no clear record of its position, the South Middleborough Church was likely a strong opponent of slavery, the traditional position of most Reformed Methodist churches. The outbreak of civil war in early 1861 had little long-term impact on South Middleborough, though a number of South Middleborough men served in the war, including John E. Smith, Ebenezer Smith, E. Howard Shaw and Simeon D. Wilbur. Residents would have kept abreast of the war news through such means as the local *Middleboro Gazette* and other locally published newspapers and would have been aware of the mounting number of causalities as the war progressed, particularly in neighboring Rock, which had a relatively high proportion of deaths in relation to the number of soldiers it sent to the front. To its great fortune, South Middleborough was largely able to escape this misery.

3

THE PEAK OF LUMBERING, 1872–1902

I'll stand by the gate and keep watching for those
Who come with the smell of pine on their clo'es.
For even in heaven I'll want it, I will,
The smell of the sawdust that comes from the mill.
—Anonymous nineteenth-century folk rhyme

Following the Civil War, Middleborough became the predominant lumber producer in the commonwealth, assuming that position as early as 1880. To South Middleborough must be credited much of the responsibility for this development. During this era, the South Middleborough community would establish a seasonal economic and corresponding social routine based on the crops produced, including white pine. Spring planting was followed by haymaking in late June and July, cranberry harvesting and screening in September and October, winter sawing during the months from November through the following June and ice harvesting traditionally in January and February.

Yet despite South Middleborough's integration within a wider economic market, economic stability coupled with a peripheral geographic location within Middleborough as a whole would continue to foster an individualistic and self-reliant ethic among the community, so much so that it sought to separate itself from Middleborough during the last quarter of the nineteenth century in the belief that it could manage its own affairs better and at lesser expense. South Middleborough would be slow in emerging from its agriculturally based economy and, because of this, often found itself the object of criticism by outsiders as "backward," conservative and not forward-thinking, particularly in regard to its attitude toward land usage.

SOUTH MIDDLEBOROUGH'S SUCCESS AS A LUMBERING CENTER

South Middleborough's late nineteenth-century mills literally consumed thousands upon thousands of pine trees harvested from South Middleborough woodlots, as well as those in neighboring communities. The ready availability of lumber at Middleborough center, much of it felled in South Middleborough, led locals to boast that "you can buy your lumber cheaper in Middleboro than in Taunton or Neponset" (two well-known lumber markets in eastern Massachusetts). The national post–Civil War expansion demanded enormous quantities of lumber, and white pine harvested locally became a valuable commodity much in demand. By 1881, according to the local *Gazette*, "the manufacturing establishments of the south part of the town are so driven that they run on holidays."

The ability of South Middleborough mills to meet this demand bore formidable results. Within four years, Middleborough had achieved the top rank in the commonwealth, producing more than twice as much lumber as its nearest competitor, a large proportion of which was milled at South Middleborough. In 1886, it was reported that "the business of cutting and teaming logs and wood to the railroads is very brisk in South Middleboro," and during the following year, over two thousand cords of un-milled wood were shipped from the South Middleborough depot. Much of South Middleborough's success in the field of forestry was based on the realization of the value of white pine and the reforestation of the town's wastelands with that rapidly maturing tree. The white pine grew well in poor soil conditions, for which South Middleborough was eminently suited.

The key to South Middleborough's profitable exploitation of its resources remained the railroad. South Middleborough became an important transit point for local lumber mill owners, and as early as November 1872, the siding of the South Middleborough station had to be lengthened "to accommodate more fully the freight business of that place." Particularly at the peak of

To access South Middleborough's vast woodlands, residents throughout the centuries cut roads through the thick vegetation and swamps. Herbert L. Wilber was so proud of the mile-long woods road he completed in August 1936 that he "took a picture of the first load out. The first motor car to ever penetrate to this lot since time began." *Courtesy of Middleborough Historical Association.*

lumbering in South Middleborough, the South Middleborough depot would prove particularly advantageous. As previously noted, in December 1886, the teaming of logs and wood to the station was reported to be very brisk, and the following year some 2,077 cords of wood alone were shipped from the South Middleborough depot. The station relied, also, on sawmills outside South Middleborough to provide a heavy volume of freight, including Hoyle's Mill in Carver.

The heavy freighting through South Middleborough had increased such that by the final decade of the century, concerns over the inadequacy of the existing freight house were mounting. In 1892, local residents were complaining that the freight house dating from the 1840s was too small and in poor repair and were demanding the construction of a new one prior to the fall cranberry shipments. Six years would pass, however, before a new freight house would be built (in 1898) on the south side of the railroad tracks opposite the depot building. Principal goods shipped through this building continued to include slabs, lumber and boxes from the local sawmills and barrels of cranberries.

Despite the volume of freight that passed through it, since its inception the South Middleborough station had struggled to remain open. Following the Civil War, the railroad wished to close both South Middleborough and Rock stations and create a new station midway between the two points. The Massachusetts Board of Railroad Commissioners, however, refused to approve the proposal, arguing that "it violently disturbs the customs, business relations and arrangements which have grown up during twenty years, and must be dismissed as impracticable." Eventually, in 1902, South Middleborough, along with the station at Rock, became a flag station; trains would no longer stop unless flagged to do so.

Ironically, while South Middleborough residents were eager to see improvement of their rail facilities, they opposed proposals for any further railroad extensions, regarding them as a threat to the local station's monopoly on freight traffic originating in the region. As early as April 1854, the Plymouth and Wareham Railroad Company was incorporated to lay a line from Plymouth to Tremont. A later proposed line through Carver, linking the Old Colony stations at Plympton and Tremont, would have deprived South Middleborough of a considerable share of its traffic originating in Carver. Neither proposal reached fruition, undoubtedly much to the relief of South Middleborough residents.

The Daily Life of Lumbering

South Middleborough's resources of standing timber were maintained in variously sized woodlots, some owned by generations of the same family, though many were acquired by local mill proprietors as lumbering advanced as an industrial activity. Land sales frequently exempted standing timber from the purchase, with grantors reserving the right to harvest. In May 1859, when Robert and Susan Rider mortgaged sixty-five acres of woodland on Pine Street, it was "agreed that no wood is to be cut on the…lots while this mortgage is in force." To access these frequently isolated stands, woods roads were cut through the forests, and lumbering at South Middleborough left its physical mark in the form of these numerous roads that today crisscross the woods of the South Purchase.

It is not readily clear what practices South Middleborough lumbermen followed in cutting their forests, though inferences may be drawn from practices elsewhere in Middleborough. Some may have engaged in clear-cutting, wherein all standing timber was removed, and farmers relied on the distribution of seed prior to and during the course of felling to reseed their lots. The advantage of this method was the production of even-aged forests and its relative cheapness when compared to other methods of seeding. Alternatively, and more likely, some may have followed the seed tree method of propagation whereby a certain number of pines were left standing within a prescribed area in order to naturally reseed the area. Such trees became known as "cabbage pines." According to one local lumberman of the period, this was the method favored by Charles N. Atwood of Rock, a large timber owner and mill operator. "He never seeded a lot but oftentimes leaves trees to seed the land." It is only natural to assume that he had acquired the practice from having witnessed it earlier at South Middleborough.

Records indicate that French Canadians, known locally simply as "French," were responsible for a large part of the timber harvesting. Several other references to the French at South Middleborough indicate their presence and, specifically, their role in felling timber. One such reference suggests that these woodcutters resided in cabins on the woodlots at South Middleborough rather than with families in the community. Most, though not all, were itinerant, and some would ultimately join the community, including Charles LeGarde, a native of Québec who was first engaged as a logger before becoming a farmer at South Middleborough.

Once felled, trees would be stripped of their limbs on site, with the resulting refuse or "slash" being left behind. Such a practice was widely resorted to at South Middleborough, where one recently cut tract in June 1909 was described as "covered with pine boughs and other refuse from the logs." Though the practice of limbing trees in the field was common, it was also potentially hazardous as the accumulated dry slash provided ready fuel for forest fires. In 1914, the commonwealth passed the so-called Slash Law, "which required landowners and timber harvesters to treat slash left from logging by lopping it and removing it from the acres adjacent to the property lines." Slash fires, however, remained a fact of lumbering, despite the law. As late as August 29, 1941, a brush fire at South Middleborough was fueled by "slash where timber had been cut off."

Following limbing, logs were carted to the sawmills, either in wagons or on sledges during the winter by teamers engaged by the mill owners for this purpose. Despite the cold weather, teaming was conducted during the winter months when logs were easier to maneuver on the frozen, frequently snow-covered ground. At the mills, the logs would be deposited in the mill yard to await milling, which generally commenced each November and wound down for haymaking in July, though occasionally sawing could run as late as the last week of August. On those occasions, the limited window for haymaking would force the preemption of further sawing until the conclusion of haying, after which milling would recommence. In one typical report, it was recorded that in 1907, John L. Benson had to temporarily suspend his "winter" sawing "until after haymaking." In any event, once cranberry cultivation became widespread beginning in the late nineteenth century, milling needed to be completed prior to the September cranberry harvest, which would preoccupy much of the community.

At the mills, pine logs were handled by a gang of men comprising a sawyer, a joiner or "jointer," an engineer and two men to draw out the boards. At times, some mills would operate two gangs when faced with a heavy workload. First, the logs would be passed through an edger, which would trim off the bark, knots and other defects and create two parallel edges. Next, the log would be passed through a trimmer, which would cut off pieces of various lengths. The sawyer operated the saw carriage and the band saw, which traveled at nine hundred feet per minute. Once sawn, the lumber would be graded and sorted, stacked in separate piles and left to season anywhere from four to ten months prior to being shipped to market. Waste such as slabs (the bark-covered sides of the logs removed by the edger) and sawdust was originally disposed of, though both later found a use. Slabs were utilized to produce lath and were used as box lumber, while sawdust found use as horse bedding, packing and shipping material, ice packing and insulation for icehouses. During times of acute coal shortages, sawdust was even investigated as a fuel alternative.

Between 1872 and 1910, the peak years of lumbering at South Middleborough, three large lumber mills operated in the community with a fourth running at Fresh Meadows, engaging a large proportion of the community as teamers, mill operatives or mill or timber owners. These mills were so vital to the livelihood of South Middleborough residents that their daily operations were deemed newsworthy, and their business activities were chronicled with regularity in the "South Middleborough" column of the *Middleboro Gazette*.

Benson's Mill (circa 1850–1915)

Benson's mill was the second oldest of the South Middleborough mills and ultimately the largest. Following the devastating South Middleborough fire of 1859, Stillman Benson erected a new sawmill on Wareham Street just north of his home. The new Benson mill was rapidly constructed during October 1860 and very much resembled the destroyed mill with the exception of its flat roof. "The Steam Mill of S. Benson & Co., South Middleboro, is fast being brought to completion. It is 35 feet by 67, two stories high above the basement. The [adjoining one-story] room containing all the machinery is to be fire proof," reported the *Namasket Gazette* at the time of the mill's construction. Attached was a sixty-five-foot-tall chimney stack on the southeast end of the building. Though the local *Gazette* speculated at the time that the mill would "probably be in running order in about one month," it was in fact not until the second week of January 1861 that it commenced operation, when it began winter sawing for the year.

The Benson mill was an important business in South Middleborough, employing in 1873 some eighteen men and paying an annual payroll of $9,600, making it comparable to the H.N. Thomas Company at Rock, another large sawmill. In 1882, the firm was known as S. Benson & Company, with Stillman Benson owning six-thirteenths of the business.

Following the 1885 death of Stillman Benson, the firm came under the control of Benson's son John S. Benson. Ultimately, John S. Benson took his own son, John L. Benson, into the firm, whereupon it became known as J.S. Benson & Son. The firm manufactured and dealt in boxboards, slabs, wood and lumber and employed ten men. Its products were "in good demand in New York, Philadelphia and other places." Given the demand for the mill's product, in the spring of 1895, Benson erected a large mill at Montello in Brockton in conjunction with a third party to manufacture boxes, with the South Middleborough mill being devoted to the sawing of logs for this purpose. The South Middleborough mill yard was in fact described in 1901 as having lumber and box logs stacked on all sides of the mill, an indication of the considerable business that it conducted.

Few physical changes were made to the mill over the years. Sometime between June 1896 and April 1901, however, a small shed for the storage of sawdust was added to the southeast corner of the building next to the chimney stack. Like other South Middleborough mill owners, the Bensons burned sawdust, as well as wood waste, to fuel their boiler. The mill was lit by kerosene lamps and portentously, like other South Middleborough mills, was without fire protection.

While sawing was conducted on the first floor, the second floor of the mill was used for a variety of purposes. After having been vacant for several years, in 1907 Lothrop A. Hayden was manufacturing cranberry separators there. Hayden's separators, developed by him and patented in 1912, were designed to separate the good from the bad cranberries that had been dry picked. Benson may have continued a similar operation on his own, for in August 1910, it was reported that he had the contract to supply the United Cape Cod Cranberry Company with screens and separators for its new screen and shipping house at South Hanson. By 1914, the upper floor of the mill was once again vacant and was subsequently occupied by the newly formed South Middleborough Grange.

The final years of the Benson mill were troubled financially. In 1909, the mill became embroiled in the collapse of Clark & Cole, a large lumber milling concern located at Middleborough center. A large creditor of Clark & Cole, J.L. Benson & Company, was unable to pay its own debts when money due it from the Middleborough mill was not forthcoming. Accordingly, J.L. Benson & Company itself was compelled to file for bankruptcy on January 12, 1910, with both Benson and his mother being forced to file for personal bankruptcy as well. Ultimately, Benson weathered the financial crisis. The property was reacquired in the name of Benson's wife, Kate, and the mill operated until it was destroyed by fire in 1915.

WITHAM'S MILL (1872–1909)

At the opposite end of the village was situated the Witham mill, which was established in May 1872 when James H. Marvel sold a parcel of vacant land just south of his house (near the intersection of present-day Wareham and Spruce Streets) to Curtis Gammons of South Middleborough and Perez H.B. Shaw, Ansel R. Churchill and B. Sears of Carver "for the purpose of building a manufacturing establishment." A steam-powered sawmill was erected shortly thereafter for the manufacture of trunks, a business that had proved lucrative in Middleborough center and previously in South Middleborough for Benson & Smith. The raising of Gammons's mill was truly a community affair and one that was excused from the traditional temperance strictures that pervaded the community, as reported by the *Old Colony Memorial*. "The old customs are not all dead. At the raising of a new box and board mill in South Middleboro, a short time since, intoxicating liquor was furnished freely to workmen and residents of the village who assisted."

The mill subsequently passed through a succession of owners, including a partnership of Curtis Gammons, Stillman Benson and the Thomas family (1877–79) and Benjamin F. Leonard of Carver (1879–84). During Leonard's ownership, the property consisted of the saw- and boxboard mill, as well as a storage building undoubtedly for housing goods awaiting shipment, including trunks that were reportedly still being manufactured. The Leonard mill was particularly known for its productivity. "The sawyer at Leonard's mill, South Middleboro, averages about 7,000 feet of lumber per day," noted one report from the period. Leonard operated the mill until his death just a few years later, following which Simeon D. Wilbur owned it for a very short period of time (two and a half months), selling it on February 6, 1884, to John Witham of South Middleborough and Witham's son, Edwin F. Witham. Under the

Edwin F. Witham (1859–1921) was prominent in the lumber trade at South Middleborough for many years and was a recognized authority in assessing the value of standing timber. Active in local political and financial circles, Witham served as a Middleborough selectman and assessor, overseer of the poor, trustee of the Middleborough Savings Bank and director of the Middleborough Cooperative Bank. *Courtesy of Middleborough Historical Association.*

Withams' ownership, the mill would become one of South Middleborough's most productive.

Like their predecessors, the Withams initially manufactured finished trunks at the plant for a period of four years in addition to producing boxboards. In September 1886, the Witham mill was producing sixty dozen trunks daily and had sawn out 1.4 million boxboards in its last run. About 1889, Edwin Witham discontinued the manufacture of trunks and began focusing exclusively on milling lumber "obtained within the vicinity from five to six miles, by his own teams." Witham would acquire numerous woodlots throughout the area, which furnished the timber that fed the mill. At the time, the firm was producing some 2.5 million boxboards annually, an amount valued at $20,000. To produce this output, an average of twenty men were employed in the two-story wood-frame mill building, which measured twenty-five by fifty feet. Among them were Curtis Gammons's brother Ephraim and John McFarlin who, together in February 1897, sawed and jointed one thousand feet of boards in just twenty-five minutes, a remarkable record. Through ownership and operation of the mill, Edwin Witham acquired a thorough knowledge of lumber milling and came to be regarded as "an especially competent judge of woodland values."

The mill building itself was described in May 1891 as a two-and-a-half-story structure with a smaller one-story engine house attached, housing the mill's boiler, which was fueled by sawdust. Adjacent was a smokestack that was replaced in January 1895. The mill was lit by kerosene lamps and was unheated. Like other mills in the vicinity, little thought was given to fire prevention, with no watchman engaged and no fire apparatus present. It is not surprising, then, that in the summer of 1895, the Witham mill was destroyed by fire. The *Middleboro Gazette* reported:

> *At about five o'clock Thursday morning, fire was discovered in Witham's mill, but before anyone could reach it the fire had got under such headway it was beyond control, and in an hour was burned to the ground. We are very sorry for Mr. Witham's loss, and for those employed there.*

Following the fire, J.S. Benson & Son, along with Clark & Cole, the lumber milling concern at Middleborough center, reportedly purchased "the material left after the burning" of the mill. Witham, despite the loss, continued the business and quickly rebuilt the mill on the same site.

In November 1902, Witham took into partnership George H. Vaughan and Foster E. Hatch of South Middleborough. Hatch did not remain with the firm long, departing in June 1904. Following Hatch's departure, the mill was plagued by periodic shutdowns. In early 1907, the mill was twice shut due to a lack of dry fuel to power the boiler, while April, May and November 1908 witnessed shutdowns because of shortages of logs.

In 1907, Witham retired from public and business life. In September of that year, probably sensing the coming local decline of the lumber milling industry, he disposed of his interest in the mill he had owned for twenty-three years to Vaughan, the sole remaining partner (Witham's father having died previously).

Vaughan's ownership of the mill was plagued with trouble. In January 1909, the mill was leveled by a spectacular fire of suspicious origin. The mill had been subject to earlier fires besides the 1895 fire that had consumed the original mill. In May 1906, the mill only "narrowly" escaped destruction when soot in its chimney stack ignited, and a September 1907 fire was extinguished as well before it could do great damage. In the 1909 fire, "the machinery and building were entirely ruined, and the loss is about $1,000. There had been no fire in the boilers for the last few days, no one was working at the mill yesterday, and the cause of the blaze is a mystery. The authorities," noted the *Middleboro Gazette*, "are conducting an investigation."

Though the mill had been destroyed, Vaughan attempted to keep his crew employed, shipping the milled boards that had survived the blaze and hauling the firm's remaining logs to the Gammons & Hunt mill at the opposite end of the village. Though the supposition was that the Vaughan mill was to be rebuilt, it never was; the grisly suicide of George Vaughan in 1910 precluded that outcome. In time, nature overtook the mill site. In early 1911, Ansel Wilbur was busy burning "splints" around the old mill site, the people "getting well smoked."

Gammons & Hunt (1902–1924)

Despite the eventual decline of lumber milling, which accelerated after 1910, as late as 1902, local prospects for the industry remained bright, resulting in the construction of the Gammons & Hunt mill near Houdlett's Corner—the intersection of Wareham and Pine Streets. The construction of Ephraim

E. H. Gammons

(Successor to J. S. BENSON & SON.)

MANUFACTURER OF

BOX BOARDS.

SLABS and SAWDUST FOR SALE. Agent for E. C. Smith & Co., Brooklyn, N. Y.

Factory and Residence, Wareham St., So. Middleboro.

Ephraim H. Gammons (1845–1926) learned the lumber trade as an employee in South Middleborough's several sawmills. In 1898, he entered business for himself at Benson's Sawmill, later forming a partnership with Charles E. Hunt and constructing a new sawmill at Houdlett's Corner (the intersection of Wareham and Pine Streets). Gammons remained in partnership with Hunt until December 1910, when he retired from the business.

H. Gammons and Charles E. Hunt's sawmill was announced in the pages of the *Middleboro Gazette*: "It is reported that another mill for sawing box boards will be built before the winter sets in South Middleboro." Gammons had extensive practical experience in lumbering and milling, having been employed in the community's various mills since his youth. He engaged in business for himself first in 1898 prior to entering into partnership with Hunt in 1902.

One of the firm's earliest and largest clients was E.C. Smith of New York, which was receiving shipments of boards from the firm by vessel from 1905 or earlier through as late as 1910. In March 1908, Gammons & Hunt shipped 600,000 boards to Smith in the course of one week. (Smith had previously been purchasing from the Witham mill since as early as 1895).

In early 1909, the mill entered a new line of production when Hunt and Edward C. Reed (who succeeded Gammons as a partner in the firm) built an addition to the mill to turn out rolls from various types of hardwood. Rolls were cylindrically shaped logs that were employed by shipyards and industry as rollers to move oversized objects. The rolls may have been produced from northern hornbeam, an exceptionally dense hardwood, and

At his death, Charles E. Hunt (1865–1942) was described as a "retired boxmaker." The son of Reverend Ephraim A. Hunt, Charles E. Hunt was engaged for many years in the local lumber industry; he was owner of the mill at Houdlett's Corner, which produced milled lumber and manufactured boxes and where Hunt himself worked as the engineer. He resided on Locust Street in the Smith-LeBaron-Hunt House. *Courtesy of Middleborough Historical Association.*

the discovery of numerous stands of this tree in the swampy lands of South Middleborough during the construction of Route 25 lends credence to the argument that this was the wood used by the Hunt mill. Rolls would have been manufactured by the mill in various lengths and diameters on large lathes. About this time, the crew consisted of "Lothrop Hayden, sawyer; Mr. Richards, jointer; Charles E. Hunt, engineer; Robert Clinton rolls in the logs; William Reed and William Wilcox draw out and stack the boards." That winter, Ralph Tripp, Chester E. Smith and Frank Russell were engaged by Hunt to cut logs. The mill was additionally busy at this time, following the destruction of George H. Vaughan's mill in January 1909, when Vaughan was utilizing the facilities here to cut and saw his logs—yet another instance of South Middleborough's community spirit.

The Gammons & Hunt Mill was the last surviving sawmill at South Middleborough proper and was able to weather the decline in local lumber milling by moving into the box log market. However, despite rising prices for logs, expenses involved in harvesting and transporting logs drastically reduced the profits gleaned by the industry as indicated by this quote from January 1918: "The price of box logs seem to be soaring, which is of course good news to the seller, although not as much profit as would at first be thought, as cutting and carting are much more than former years." The rise in box log prices at the time was partially driven by a coal shortage in the midst of World War I, as had been the case in 1903. "The dealers in wood are reaping a harvest, and prices have been quoted as high as $14 per cord for sawed, dry wood. Indeed, it might safely be said that this is the first time that a dealer could cut his wood, load it on the wagon and deliver it the same or next day and get his price."

The Hunt Mill, like its predecessors at South Middleborough, was ultimately destroyed by fire, a blaze consuming the mill early on Sunday evening, April 27, 1924. Hunt chose not to rebuild, most likely discouraged by the poor market for wood, and his decision marked the true end of lumbering in the heart of South Middleborough, despite the fact that Century Lumber would operate here in the 1960s and 1970s.

FRESH MEADOWS SAWMILL (CIRCA 1734–1963)

The oldest and longest lived of all the sawmills at South Middleborough, however, was the Fresh Meadows sawmill, which was long powered by the Weweantic River. Industrial activity at Fresh Meadows dated as far back as May 1734, when a sawmill is mentioned as being located on the site. The sawmill was located in Middleborough at the southern end of the dam that straddled the Weweantic between Middleborough and Carver. The operation of a sawmill at Fresh Meadows was an important early development for the area of South Middleborough and adjoining South Carver as it enabled settlers to construct homes of sawn lumber.

In time, the sawmill and industrial works at Fresh Meadows came to be owned by Abigail (Weston) Wood, wife of Horatio Wood. When the Woods sold the property in 1846, it consisted of "a dwelling house, barn, store, forge tools and implements." William B. Gibbs acquired the property and, between 1846 and 1848, would seem to have constructed a board, stave and shingle mill combined in a single building. Between 1848 and 1876, the mills would be owned and operated in a partnership with Gibbs, Eleazer Richmond, James H. Look, Nathan Ryder, Robert Rider, Lewis Kinney, Lothrop Shurtleff, Harrison Hall and Linus Ryder all participating.

Eventually, by 1876, ownership of the mill operations—including the board, stave and shingle mill, a second smaller shingle mill, the up-and-down sawmill, the land and the dam—was consolidated by Nathaniel S. Cushing, a resident of East Street. South Carver poet John Maxim, who wrote under the pseudonym "Bemis," left behind a bit of doggerel from the time of Cushing's ownership of the Fresh Meadow mill:

Cushing's mill is running still,
And in it work two souls;
The joiner's name I have forgot
The sawyer's name is Bowles.

Cushing owned the mill until 1925, at which time he sold it to Harrison F. Shurtleff. The mill was later operated following 1945 by Nathaniel F. Shurtleff and later by his son, Richard. The ancient sawmill was destroyed in a fire in March 1963, although remnants of the operation may still be seen at the site.

The Life of the Lumberman

For those engaged in it, lumbering was an arduous, often miserable, frequently dangerous and financially unrewarding occupation. The task of felling trees in the woods often proved dangerous, and a number of accounts of trees falling on unsuspecting woodcutters at South Middleborough are on record. Not on record are the probably equally numerous "narrow escapes." Teaming, though perhaps moderately safer, could be dreary and difficult, conducted as it was during the coldest winter months when logs moved more easily on frozen, snow-covered ground. Warmer weather made the situation worse, as acknowledged by the local *Gazette*: "So many rains make it bad for teaming, filling the swamps with water." Further, though teamers frequently worked as independent contractors unconnected with the mills, teaming was generally not financially remunerative. In January 1907, Fred P. Hall abandoned teaming because of its low wages and went to work in Benson's sawmill. Similarly, Edward Sisson, in late winter 1908, purchased a heavy draft horse for carting logs but gave up the business within a matter of days, "finding out that there was not a chance to make himself rich at the present time, in teaming."

For those men engaged in cutting and milling timber, their job could prove extremely hazardous, if not fatal. The most notorious example of this dangerous aspect of milling was the 1883 death of Robert B. Hatch of South Middleborough, which was reported in the Plymouth *Old Colony Memorial.* "While at work sawing boards in Benson's mill, [Hatch] was struck by a piece of lumber which flew from the saw and fatally injured." Though such deaths fortunately were rare, injuries were not, and numerous cases of crushed or lacerated appendages were recorded. Frequently, such injuries might keep mill operatives from work, temporarily or even permanently.

Besides the often debilitating physical and psychological effects of lumbering, there were its economic consequences. The lumber industry engaged a relatively large proportion of the community's small populace, promoting an unhealthy economic dependence on lumbering for providing many of the community's members with a livelihood. The growth of lumbering at South Middleborough created, in essence, a one-industry economy with few economic opportunities or little reprieve for its members beyond lumbering or farming. Such a lack of opportunity is well illustrated

Despite the prominence of the Witham Mill in the economic life of South Middleborough, there remains little visual documentation of it. Here the mill proper is glimpsed in the background, while the small engine room, with its towering chimney, is closest to the viewer. Wood slabs stand stacked to the left to season. Though the men are unidentified, the horse belonged to William H. Thomas, who worked as a teamster.

in the career of Roswell D. Houdlett, who resided at the southern end of the village at the intersection of Wareham and Pine Streets, known, appropriately enough, as Houdlett's Corner. In late March 1911, Houdlett quit his job as a teamster with John L. Benson, which he had held for a long time, because (understandably) "he could not stand the work as teamer any longer." Despite the *Middleboro Gazette*'s belief that Houdlett would no "doubt find plenty of easier work than loading logs," he didn't. Within a month, Houdlett had returned to work loading wood and boards for William H. Thomas and by Labor Day was back in Benson's employment, "at his usual occupation of driving team." Such was the fate of South Middleborough's unskilled laborers.

Lumbering, because of its seasonal nature, was also economically difficult on lumbermen, particularly at South Middleborough, where mills were traditionally idle during the summer months. While mill employees could usually find jobs assisting farmers in order to carry them through the slow season, they were not always successful. Even during the sawing season, work in the mills could prove sporadic, most frequently due to shortages of logs. In April 1908, George H. Vaughan was forced to shut his mill for a few days because of a scarcity of logs. Restarted soon afterward, it was again idle within a month. Later, about one week into the following winter's season, Vaughan was once more compelled to shut down for want of logs. Such "dull times" would send South Middleborough mill operatives on enforced vacations, such as Foster E. Hatch, who was out of work from Atwood's mill in Rock during slow periods in 1908 and 1921.

Charcoal, Ice, Hay and Cranberries

While lumber milling remained the principal occupation of most South Middleborough residents, it was not the only one, and a byproduct of the lumber industry was the development of a local charcoal-making business. By the late 1800s, South Middleborough had become a large producer of charcoal, an industry literally fuelled by the abundance of local timber in the vicinity.

It is likely that the occupation originated through the local iron industry's demand for charcoal. Furnaces located nearby in Carver, as well as in Stillwater along Black Brook on the Middleborough–Rochester line, required vast amounts of charcoal to fuel their operations. The area's heavy blanket of pine and other trees made it a natural producer of charcoal to sate the demands of these local furnaces, and charcoal making had developed into a relatively significant industry by the close of the Civil War. In 1875, Middleborough as a whole was the eighth-largest producer of charcoal in Massachusetts, producing some 42,925 bushels valued at $4,932. That same year, Henry N. Maynard of Benson Street in South Middleborough developed a new process for burning charcoal whereby he was able to reduce drastically the burning time of a charcoal pit from some eighteen or twenty days to just five. Maynard was noted for his charcoal-making skills, and in December 1875, it was reported that he had "lately coaled a pit for Mr. S[tillman] Benson, that is estimated to contain a thousand bushels, and not a spark of fire was to be found when it was opened." Charcoal continued to be produced at South Middleborough following the turn of the century. In April 1906, Charles B. Cushman was burning pits for William H. Thomas, and Ellis Gibbs was similarly engaged in September 1908, charcoaling 365 cords of pine for John L. Benson (undoubtedly for use in his mill) and 45 cords for the Andrews cranberry bog.

While not a local industry at South Middleborough, per se, ice harvesting was a winter occupation for many in the area, especially during the months of January and February. Roswell Houdlett, Lyman P. Thomas, William Shaw, William Bearse, Ansel C. Wilbur and Ira A. Porter all had icehouses, and it is likely that other residents did as well. Among the various lumber mills, Gammons & Hunt was noted for operating an icehouse, too. Many of these icehouses dated from just following the turn of the century; Houdlett's was built in 1907 by James B. Tripp, while Thomas's "large ice house" was built the following winter. Among those who harvested ice, Thomas appears to have been the only one who marketed it commercially to any extent. In February 1909, he had housed some 150 tons of nine-inch ice, and the following month, he purchased additional ice in order to fill the house to capacity. By mid-August, however, the ice was nearly depleted, and he was compelled to purchase more.

Yet another large South Middleborough agricultural crop during the nineteenth century was hay. Though lumbering remained the principal occupation for many at South Middleborough, haying was the one task that could preempt "winter" sawing, so critical was it to harvest the hay when the weather was advantageous. The need to harvest the crop quickly in between showers and periods of wet weather required many hands, which in some years were not available. During 1917, haymakers were busy with a large

Rock-strewn and relatively sandy soil prevented the development of agriculture on an extensive scale in South Middleborough, though hay was easily grown. Hay remained one of the largest crops propagated in both South Middleborough and neighboring Rock in the early twentieth century, as indicated by this photograph of a young Dura Higgins. *Courtesy of Sharon Higgins Cope-Carriere.*

crop but found labor scarce as the nation began preparing for war. Hay was always a favored crop at South Middleborough since the generally poor soil of the district was conducive to little else. There is little mention of what types of hay were cultivated in South Middleborough, though a 1919 record mentions "quite a crop of rowen."

Despite the modern-day prevalence of cranberry bogs throughout the region, South Middleborough was a relative latecomer to cranberry cultivation, despite its suitability for the crop. One of the earliest bogs in South Middleborough was that of Frank Short, who purchased two adjoining tracts of land totaling forty-seven acres in 1894 and 1898 from John S. and John L. Benson located at Houdlett's Corner. Short subsequently drained twenty-five of these acres and transformed them into a cranberry bog.

Following 1895, others began constructing bogs as well, encouraged by high prices paid for the crop and the ready availability of suitable land. The area experienced a boom in bog building during the first decade of the new century, and by 1905–06, Lyman P. Thomas and Ephraim H. Gammons were involved in cranberry cultivation. Thomas's bog was located to the rear of his house and was expanded in June 1905 and again during the spring of 1909. Additional bogs were proposed in April 1907 by Thomas and Short and, in March 1909, by William H. Thomas. Also in 1909, the Silverberg Bog was constructed on Wareham Street near the Rochester line by Gustav and August Silverberg of Wareham. Sometime in the early 1900s, Lothrop Hayden constructed a small cranberry bog on the south side of Pine Street, which he sold in 1908 to Andrew Kaski of Carver. John

Among the cranberry pickers engaged on the bog of Marcus Atwood in South Carver about September 1900 were a number of South Middleborough residents. *Front, left to right*: ----- Atwood, Louise (Wilbur) Higgins, Ellis Atwood, Ethel (Smith) Barrows, Clarence Wilbur, Herbert Wilber and Ansel C. Wilbur; *Middle*: Elva Atwood, Dolly Atwood, Rose Atwood, Charlie Kennedy, Frank Atwood, Frank Smith, Mrs. Frank Smith and Simeon D. Wilbur; *Back*: Stephen Dexter Atwood, Mrs. S. Dexter Atwood, Marcus Atwood, Madella McFarlin, Mary Wilbur, Nellie B. (Wilbur) Porter and Ruth Raymond. *Courtesy of Middleborough Historical Association.*

Feltch was also engaged in cranberrying and is recorded in October 1907 as having his berries screened.

The establishment of an active cranberry industry in South Middleborough had several consequences. Economically, cranberrying provided an alternative to lumbering and thereby softened the financial consequences of the decline in the latter industry. Shipping of berries on both the railroad and the electric car lines helped support those operations, which continued to also provide valuable passenger service to the area. Additionally, cranberry cultivation encouraged the development of ancillary industries that grew from previously established lumber mills. John Benson began making cranberry screens, while Lothrop Hayden established a separator manufactory in the space above Benson's mill. Socially, the industry wrought changes as well, providing employment to South Middleborough residents, including women, who previously had found little work outside the home. Many would be engaged annually to screen the berries during the fall harvest. Additionally, much to their delight, local schoolchildren were frequently absented from classes in September in order to assist with the fall harvest.

Huckleberries

Prior to the propagation of cranberries, South Middleborough's principal fruit crop had been the wild huckleberry. Though never a crop of enormous commercial value for South Middleborough, huckleberries figured prominently in the social history of the community, and references to huckleberrying appeared frequently in the period preceding the First World War.

The wild huckleberry was noted in the earliest written accounts of the region made by European explorers. About 1602, Captain John Smith had described nearby Cape Cod as "overgrown with shrubby pines, hirts [huckleberries], and such trash." Areas closer to South Middleborough were likewise marked for their "considerable undergrowth of vines, huckleberry bushes and other shrubby plants." Huckleberries thrived in both the swamps and uplands of South Middleborough, and they grew there in such abundance that they gave their name to nearby Huckleberry Corner in Carver, where residents would sell their berries to the occupants of passing stages.

Wild huckleberries were picked for sale throughout the last decades of the nineteenth century. In 1875, Middleborough produced 4,756 quarts of the berry valued at $421, a not inconsiderable amount when contrasted with the value of Middleborough's other agricultural output at the time. The *Gazette*, noting the local sales from its woods and dairy farms, remarked, "Only think of the bowls of huckleberries and milk."

Attempts were made in South Middleborough, as elsewhere, to commercially exploit this natural bounty, and in July 1885, an unnamed South Middleborough man was in fact shipping several crates of huckleberries a week to Nantucket, reportedly "doing a good business…and realizing good prices." However, because the huckleberry plant was wild and had yet been domesticated, harvests were highly dependent on the vagaries of nature.

Huckleberrying remained a social activity for many South Middleborough residents throughout the period when large numbers took to the woods in search of the berry. "The huckleberry swamps have been well visited for the past week," noted the *Middleboro Gazette* in July 1895, "and must be pretty well stripped of ripe fruit." An entry in the diary of Herbert L. Wilber in September 1916 records the social nature of South Middleborough huckleberrying:

> *This afternoon I picked huckleberries.* [Herbert's brother] *Alden went and had the thoughtfulness to bring in Herman Russell, and the consequence was they cleaned out that poor little place in short order.*
>
> *Aunt Nellie* [Porter] *came in, too, towards the last and helped to find a place for those scared huckleberries to hide. I had a bridal veil of cloth gauze to ward off the noxious things that fly; and I needed it before I got through. Aunt N. went home at four. I lost several good minutes to make sure that she got on the road and started in the right direction, for I remember once that I left for home early and she wandered off and got lost. She was nearly purple with the heat too, and wanted to know if I was going home too. I nobly scoffed at the idea of leaving while there was room in my pails* [capacity thirteen quarts].
>
> *I said I was going to search for berries the other side of the road. She said that there were no berries there for she had looked, and that proved it. However, I remembered that thought can do anything, and I believed I could find berries there.*
>
> *So I did within a stone's throw of the argument: some of the very best of picking. I got 3 qts. and left some that it was too dark to see…When I arrived home my wife was greatly disappointed because she had it all settled*

> *that I was lost in the woods, and when she read this account she thought I must have gone crazy with the heat. A thunderstorm is brewing. I picked 11 qts. of berries, so help me.*

Postbellum Commerce

Fueled by the growth of its local lumber industry and with a strong agricultural foundation, South Middleborough continued to progress following the Civil War, with 1867 being noted by the local *Middleboro Gazette* as a particularly noteworthy year:

> *Within the past year the people of South Middleboro have perhaps made as much progress in spiritual, and temporal things as any part of the town according to the number of inhabitants…A new parsonage has been purchased and now they are establishing a union store. Their motto is onward and upward.*

The union store mentioned by the local newspaper was that of James M. Clark, who by 1867 had successfully consolidated the earlier mercantile interests of South Middleborough into a single operation housed in his home at Clark's Corner. In 1873, Clark retired from the grocery business, and in November of that year, he turned the store over to his son, James M. Clark Jr. According to Jennie Gammons, local customers were initially less accommodating to the younger Clark than they had been to his father:

> *Customers found fault with the slightest mistake, scarcely mentioned under the captain's management. Complaints were made if there was a shortage of a particular product wanted. Commodities were weighed out as called for and a sharp watch of the scales was necessary. Short weight made trouble and overweight was a loss to the grocer…He dabbled in lard, sugar, butter and what not until he learned how a pound of stuff looked. Molasses was a mess drawn from a barrel by a faucet and invariably left a sticky pool on the floor. Kerosene, always in demand, was just as bad, and spilled over to leave an odor. In addition to groceries, there was a line of dry goods and small wares, pins, needles, thread, cotton cloth, calico, everything for the country housewife. The list to keep in stock made his head swim. Accurate*

> *accounts were to be kept daily. If the ledger showed signs of dropping into the red, there was cause for alarm.*

The younger Clark, however, was able to surmount these difficulties and within three years' time was able to engage an assistant, enabling the store to solicit trade beyond South Middleborough. "His horse-drawn vehicle became a familiar figure on country roads for miles." Successful solicitation of trade permitted the assistant clerk to become full time and another to be hired.

Clark also became South Middleborough's postmaster, and the post office was established in the store. Mail pouches were brought daily from the South Middleborough station and deposited at the store, where mail would be sorted into a homemade wooden rack that was nailed to a wall behind the counter "almost out of sight." The layout of the operation was described by Jennie Gammons:

Between 1846 and 1935, South Middleborough maintained a post office, the very existence of which identified the area as a separate and distinct community. One of the most tangible identifiers of South Middleborough was the postmark, which cancelled the postage of all mail originating in the local post office. For most of the period until 1892, the office was located inside the South Middleborough store.

> *A counter at the right of the entrance catered mostly to feminine trade, wall shelves supplied cotton goods, calicoes, ginghams and small wares for sewing. At the further end the U.S. Post Office snuggled in its berth and postage stamps were sold over the counter. At the counter on the left, commodities were weighed out while the customer looked on to verify the correct balance.*

Bulk goods like molasses, kerosene, flour and grain were stored in the back room. The store remained in the Clark House until 1892, when it moved across what is now Locust Street to larger accommodations.

A second noteworthy commercial enterprise established at this time was the South Middleborough blacksmith shop, which was built about 1874 on present-day Locust Street and owned by Stillman Benson and William H. Thomas. It seems the two men constructed the shop in order to lease it as a business venture. During the 1870s, Edward H. Cromwell of Rochester served as the blacksmith, followed by Allen Chamberlain, who quit in 1886 due to ill health. At the time Chamberlain left smithing, the shop was acquired by Edward E. Sisson, whose "name will ever be associated with that of village blacksmith" of South Middleborough.

Complementing the work of the South Middleborough blacksmith shop was Henry H. Shaw's livery stable, which operated out of the barn at the former Baptist Parsonage on Spruce Street. The business probably terminated after a short time, as there was little call for a livery operation at South Middleborough, where residents already owned horses and visitors were infrequent.

Sisson served as South Middleborough's blacksmith from 1886 until 1920, having learned the trade from Luther Reynolds of Acushnet, and the Sisson blacksmith shop was a busy one, serving as it did a wide area. In one week alone in February 1905, Sisson shod fifty-seven horses and two yoke of oxen. Because of steady business, Sisson employed a number of assistants over the years, including Rufus T. Benson, William G. Hayne or Haney and Frank Delano.

Following 1905, declining health prompted Sisson to take what would be the first of several health-related breaks from blacksmithing, an indication of the arduousness of the job. In October 1909, Sisson reported experiencing back problems; four years later, in October 1913, he was severely kicked in the knee while shoeing. Working essentially outdoors caused physical problems as well. In March 1914, Sisson became sick with a severe cold after "a very busy day with so many shoeing and sharpening of horses."

And the work continued. During both February 1917 and January 1918, Sisson was reportedly very busy sharpening horseshoes because of the icy roads. In January 1918, he once more hurt his back. An August 1918 bout of tonsillitis, followed by a subsequent illness the following December, prompted Sisson to close the shop, forcing local residents to travel either to Middleborough center or Tremont for blacksmithing work. In March 1920, after thirty-four years as South Middleborough's blacksmith, Sisson gave up the occupation.

SOUTH MIDDLEBOROUGH SCHOOL

In addition to these commercial enterprises, the community's advancement was further demonstrated by the construction of a new schoolhouse in 1882. While an earlier school had been built at South Middleborough in the vicinity of the 1882 South Middleborough School and appears to have been standing in the late 1700s, little is known of that building. Later, what was probably a second school for South Middleborough was erected at Houdlett's Corner. Sadly, the South Middleborough School there appears not to have been well maintained. In 1881, the Middleborough School Committee of Warren H. Southworth, Nathan T. Dyer and James F. Shurtleff was scathing in its appraisal of the school's physical deficiencies. Not surprisingly, given the strong criticism of the South Middleborough schoolhouse, the Town of Middleborough voted the following year to replace it, selecting a new site opposite the Methodist church "believed to be the one best adapted and most conveniently located" for the pupils, purchasing it from Chandler R. Smith in May 1882 for forty dollars. The old South Middleborough School was sold for eighty-five dollars and moved across Wareham Street, where it was incorporated into the Shaw House.

The South Middleborough School was completed in 1882 at a cost of $1,233.30 and was recognized at the time as a thoroughly modern schoolhouse, reflective of the school committee's pronounced views on schoolhouse hygiene. For two decades, the 1882 schoolhouse served the community well. Following the turn of the century, however, as a result of the growth the community had witnessed during the past two decades, as well as the closure of the Highland School, the South Middleborough School began experiencing overcrowding, and in May 1906, the school's forty-eight seats were filled to capacity. The eventual transfer of South Middleborough's ninth grade scholars to Middleborough center would temporarily alleviate the situation, and it signaled a process of rationalization whereby the number of grades taught in South Middleborough was gradually reduced from nine to just the two that it housed when it closed in 1991.

Built in 1882, the one-room South Middleborough School was considered a model schoolhouse, though not everyone agreed with this assessment. Jennie Gammons, who was in the first class to attend school in the building, recalled in 1933 "the builder's mistake of exposing the two entrances directly to the cold, north winds, bellowing for admission every time a door opened. That bungle has produced much discomfort in the last 53 years."

POSTBELLUM SOCIAL LIFE

While economically and educationally South Middleborough may have been progressing during this era, socially it remained a quiet community where the influence of the Methodist Church was strongly felt. Temperance was encouraged, gambling frowned upon and the principal social outlets remained those affiliated with the church. Services on Sundays consisted of the prayer meeting at 9:00 a.m. followed by the sermon at 10:00 a.m. and Sunday school at noon, as well as an evening prayer service. The length of Sunday worship was not pleasing to all, and Louise (Wilbur) Higgins related the story of her grandfather Simeon D. Wilbur's brother David, who visited on weekends and attended church with the family. Finding the services interminably long, David Wilbur slipped out between the sermon and Sunday school for some

> *fresh air and was unprepared to have grandmother hunt him up and beckon him urgently toward the church door with a reminder, "Come, David, it's time for a Class meeting now." Not an habitual churchgoer, Uncle questioned in dismay, "What? Aint there no let up to this?" But he dutifully followed the faithful into the Class meeting, registering a mental vow to confine future visits to his brother to weekdays.*

The church was an important influence within the community, both religiously (as the arbiter of the community's morals and values) and socially (as the sponsor of such organizations as the Ladies' Aid Society, Epworth League, Methodist Youth Fellowship and Women's Christian Temperance Union). Among its most popular events was its annual Sunday school picnic, generally held at such venues as Onset and Bates Pond in Carver, which provided the highlight of many summers during the first decades of the twentieth century. Additionally, the vestry of the church, particularly prior to 1916, when the South Middleborough Grange Hall was constructed, was frequently the scene of important community meetings. The church also conducted well-attended Sunday school classes (the maples in front of the church date from 1928 and were planted by members of the young men's class). And while certainly not intended to be a social activity, per se, Sunday worship services, plus twice-weekly prayer meetings on Tuesday and Thursday evenings, provided an opportunity for community members to

Churchgoing remained an important feature of the South Middleborough scene through the twentieth century. At the start of the century, Sundays meant one's best clothes and hitching the horse to the wagon or buggy to ride, rather than walk, to church. Here, Ansel C. Wilbur and his family are doing just that on September 3, 1916. *Courtesy of Middleborough Historical Association.*

gather. Long afterward, "Grandma Benson," the wife of Deacon Stillman Benson, would be remembered as attending these meetings: "The slight, old lady, with bent shoulders and lantern in hand would plod along the dark, dusty road to prayer meeting." Not until the early 1900s would the Tuesday evening prayer meeting be discontinued.

The church's Epworth League was a frequent sponsor of entertainments within the community, as evidenced by its work with a concert to benefit missionary work in late 1894 and a Harvest Gathering in the autumn of 1895 that featured singing, readings, speeches and "two large barrels…filled with a variety of vegetables and canned fruits." Following the event, the food was donated to the Epworth settlement at Boston.

"Entertainments," both sacred and secular in nature, were always popular. In 1869, Charles H. Wilbur contemplated the construction of a public hall at South Middleborough, but this proposal failed to mature, and the church vestry remained the principal venue for church-sanctioned entertainments. Among these events were lectures and concerts. One series of concerts was performed by blind musician Frank Taylor, who entertained on a number of occasions. Unfortunately, Taylor failed to vary his program with each subsequent engagement so that upon his fourth visit to South Middleborough in March 1895, his audience numbered only six. "Being always about the same programme, people were not attracted by it," explained the *Gazette*. The church also sponsored *Middleboro Gazette* editor James M. Coombs, who spoke in November 1895 on the topic of newspapers.

Besides the Methodist church vestry, another venue for socials and entertainments, at least during the summer months, was LeBaron's Grove, located near the church on the land of Cyrus LeBaron, where roughly Sisson's Diner and the former South Middleboro Filling Station and Garage now stand. "The pine grove with its cathedral arch" was considered "a beauty spot of this section" and was hired for all sorts of gatherings. In September 1875, the grove

One of the oldest houses remaining at South Middleborough, the Smith-LeBaron-Hunt House on Locust Street, is believed to have been built about 1750. Between the house and the church once stood the white pine grove known as LeBaron's Grove, which was a favored locale for summer entertainments for the community. The grove was named for the mid-nineteenth-century occupant of the house, Cyrus LeBaron. *Photograph by Michael J. Maddigan.*

was the scene of another community picnic, with music by the sixteen-piece Carver band, and an exhibition in the evening. Entertainments here, too, were often dominated by both religious and patriotic overtones. The community's 1868 July Fourth picnic (which was termed "delightful" by the *Middleboro Gazette*) was presided over by Reverend Mr. Gammons and saw tables spread "with the most tempting and generous supply of edibles." For Independence Day 1877, Reverend Henry B. Hidden, chaplain of the U.S. Navy, was orator. In the summer of 1878, LeBaron's Grove hosted a gospel temperance meeting with an address by Reverend Henry M. Eaton of Millbridge, Maine.

Henry K.W. Ryder on Spruce Street also maintained a pine grove on his property that doubled as a site for local entertainments. In August 1895, a neighborhood clambake was held there, where some "hundred or more [were] served to a good dinner of baked clams, fish, potatoes and dressing, and as usual, a generous supply of pastry, ice cream following." Admission was charged, with the proceeds going to fund the purchase of a new carpet for the South Middleborough church.

While the influence of the local church on the social climate remained strong, it was not absolute, and other organizations provided South Middleborough residents with social and recreational opportunities outside the purview of the church. During the late 1880s, the South Middleboro Band was formed, and officers serving during 1889 were President Chester E. Smith, Vice-President Philander W. Southworth and Treasurer John L. Feltch, with Harvey Raymond of Carver as leader. Intellectual life was stimulated by the formation, in 1904, of a Shakespearean Club, which appears to have been short-lived. Dances were frequently held in private homes, including one "social dance" left on record from early March 1895 at the home of Charles H. Maxim. Sports, while not formally organized, remained popular, with coasting, skating and ice fishing in winter and informal games of baseball during the summers that were frequently played in Benson's "Barn Field" on Wareham Street against teams from archrival Rock Village.

Despite the religious overtones of much of South Middleborough's social life during the postbellum era, it was neither as oppressive nor as restrictive as one would perhaps believe, as indicated by a news report from the period: "An old bachelor in the south part of the town is bringing up his niece in a moral way. When he discovers her walking home with a young man from the evening meetings, he compels her to pay a fine of ten cents. They say he is making money."

ON THE PERIPHERY

Despite the economic advances made by South Middleborough throughout this period, the outlying village remained on the periphery of Middleborough, the geographic distance between South Middleborough and Middleborough center creating a corresponding economic and psychological distance. The Plymouth *Old Colony Memorial* recognized that geography was largely to blame: "The two extreme points of Middleboro are fourteen and one half miles apart in a direct line. To travel from one to another, by road, the distance is about eighteen miles."

Following 1800, the village of the Lower Four Corners in Middleborough began to emerge as the commercial, industrial, civic and social center of the town. Municipal improvements would come rapidly to Middleborough center in the form of graded schools (1850–51), municipal fire protection (1852), gas lighting (1856), house numbering (1859), sidewalks (1860s), police protection (1880s), municipal waterworks (1885), sewerage (1885), electricity (1889) and telephonic communication (1890s) but much less rapidly, if at all, to villages like South Middleborough, which learned to cope without

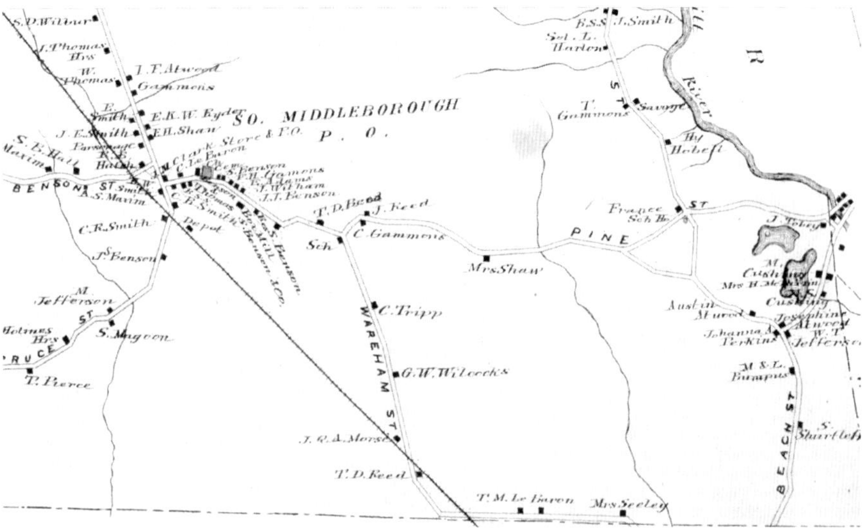

By 1879, when this map was produced, Clark's Corner was firmly entrenched as the "center" of South Middleborough. Here were located the post office and store, while nearby was the railroad depot and freight station, Methodist church and South Middleborough Cemetery. Three years later, when a new school was constructed for the community, it was not surprisingly located nearby. In 1890, the grade crossing at Benson Street was eliminated.

such amenities. As the development at Middleborough center continued, the economic disparity between the center and its outlying villages was not only solidified but also made manifest. The economic importance of Middleborough center marginalized and isolated communities like South Middleborough, which saw its interests more closely allied with neighboring communities in South Carver, North Rochester and West Wareham rather than Middleborough, which it supported through its taxation but from which it felt it derived few benefits.

The South Middleborough community had long been conditioned to think this way. During the colonial era, South Middleborough had been confessionally opposed to the established church and had only infrequent contact with Middleborough. As late as 1905, lingering resentment toward the Congregational-dominated society of the center was still latent under the surface at South Middleborough. Speaking to an audience of Methodists in that year, Matthew H. Cushing expressed admiration for the rise of Methodism at the expense of "that denomination which compelled us by the English laws to contribute to their support even by seizing our property or incarcerating our ancestors in prison."

South Middleborough residents chafed at the characterization of Middleborough's outlying villages (of which they were one) as "the hayseed district" and their depiction as conservative and unprogressive. Further, and more immediately, South Middleborough residents continually felt short-changed in terms of services and amenities they received from the town, often adopting an almost quiet resignation, accepting what was granted them. One South Middleborough correspondent, clearly aware that the level of services declined the farther one moved geographically from Middleborough center, gave voice to this resignation. Writing of the South Middleborough School, the correspondent noted that "it cannot be the most healthful of rooms, and if at the centre [of town] would be greatly criticized, but out here in the bush anything that will hold the children is considered sufficient."

Such feelings of antagonism, frustrated desire and quiet resignation, coupled with the more immediate economic issue of taxation, were the root cause of South Middleborough's efforts to separate itself from the larger town in 1884–85. Earlier efforts in 1879 to set off the southern portion of Middleborough as a separate town emanated from Rock and were driven largely by taxation issues. Though these efforts failed, the move to separate from Middleborough was renewed in the summer of 1884, this

While outsiders may have perceived South Middleborough as the "hayseed district," the Wilbur family demonstrated otherwise. Louise Wilbur (shown here in 1906) was one of four members of her family to serve as salutatorian of Middleborough High School, along with Herbert L. Wilber (1907), Ellis Wilbur (1909) and Philip Wilber (1932). Dorothy Wilber was valedictorian of the 1944 class, a remarkable accomplishment for any family. *Courtesy of Sharon Higgins Cope-Carriere.*

time at South Middleborough as reported by the *Old Colony Memorial.* "South Middleborough wants to be set off and made a new town by itself, the inhabitants thinking they can run a town government on a tax of about $10.00 per thousand."

Strangely, some commentators outside Middleborough favored the incorporation of a new town at South Middleborough. The Plymouth *Old Colony Memorial* opined that such a division could only benefit "the progress and prosperity of the old town, which is now hindered in public enterprises by some of the outlying districts not comprehending or caring for the good of the whole." Presumably, shorn of its peripheral villages, Middleborough Center would flourish. However, it was probable that neither would have benefited. It is doubtful that a separate South Middleborough would have been able to establish an effectively functioning municipal government providing services comparable to those at Middleborough center on such a low tax rate, while Middleborough center, devoid of the tax revenues from outlying residents, would have been forced to either increase its own tax rate to compensate for lost tax revenues or curtail the municipal services provided there. Ultimately it was a symbiotic relationship: each community needed the other to exist. Nonetheless, a lingering perception of being short-changed would persist at South Middleborough for years to come.

South Middleborough's Sluggish Development

Clearly, the view of South Middleborough as seen from outside the community in the years following the Civil War was somewhat unflattering; many outsiders regarded the community as insular and unprogressive. With the loss in the 1859 fire of what industry it had, South Middleborough would afterward remain a community devoted to agriculture where traditional land-based values were esteemed. However, the agricultural basis of South Middleborough's economy marked it in contrast to Middleborough as a whole, which had begun to abandon agriculture and was, by the last decade of the nineteenth century, considered to be an industrial community. "Middleboro folks certainly can lay a little claim to being farmer folk still, although if anyone asks you the business of the town you will probably answer, more or less truthfully, 'the shoe business,'" noted one late nineteenth-century commentator. However, the story was much different at South Middleborough, where, as late as 1917, "almost anyone who has a spot of land that can be conveniently used for farming [is] making the most of it."

Like elsewhere, land at South Middleborough tended to remain in the hands of single families, and farms were passed from generation to generation. The *Middleboro Gazette*, clearly cognizant of this tradition, asked in 1877, "Who ever thought of having a real estate broker in South Middleboro, where the farms have been in the same family for three or four generations?" Industry, other than lumber milling, had little incentive to locate at South Middleborough since the best railroad connections and industrially trained workers were situated in Middleborough center, which accordingly became the locus of industry in town.

Exemplifying the tradition of landholding within individual families was Hillside Farm, the home of William H. Thomas, seen here from the south in 1916, which still stands near the junction of Wareham and Spruce Streets. Built on a portion of the historic Thomas farm, it was later joined by a series of houses built for members of the same family.

Because the land at South Middleborough was either farmed or forested, the trend was toward the consolidation rather than division of parcels. Furthermore, there was no countervailing pressure toward subdivision as there was at Middleborough center, where residential building lots were greatly in demand. At South Middleborough, there was neither a need nor a desire to sell land, nor was the sale of real estate considered advisable from an economic standpoint. And in any case, there was little desire by outsiders to acquire land in South Middleborough unless it was for agricultural purposes, in which instance existing farms were generally purchased outright.

Residential development that did occur tended to be accomplished to provide family members with house lots, as was the case with the development of the Smith, Thomas and Wilbur farms, all subdivided to provide family members with building lots. This trend followed a historical tradition of family farms being subdivided for the support of family members, a tradition that stretched back to the first settlement of the region but had long since disappeared in industrially based communities such as Middleborough center. The fact that this colonial-era tradition still lingered

Henry K.W. Ryder, like other homebuilders on the east side of Spruce Street, purchased his house lot from the Reformed Methodist Society for $100 in August 1878, building this home shortly afterward. Ryder was a sawmill employee and teamster who was involved with the Epworth League and the South Middleborough Cemetery. Jennie Gammons described him as "just as odd as his name, but a faithful, kindly soul."

at South Middleborough was but one more instance where the community was open to criticism as "backward."

This is not to say that residential subdivision did not occur. Following the Civil War, the Reformed Methodist Society divested itself of a portion of its property on the northeast side of Spruce Street, resulting in the construction of houses by Ebenezer Smith (1872) and Henry K.W. Ryder (circa 1879). Other houses followed, including those for Frederick E. Braley (circa 1900), George H. Vaughan (circa 1904) and Arthur F. Nye (1909) and that of Allen Chamberlain (later Edward E. Sisson; circa 1880) on Locust Street. The Robert B. Hatch House on old Benson Street was built during the summer of 1869 for Hatch, a lumber mill operative, and its construction was noted in the Plymouth *Old Colony Memorial*: "Mr. Robert Hatch has just completed a neat cottage, near the end of Benson street, adjoining the parsonage estate, which he intends for his own residence." Similarly, Stillman Benson developed his property on the northern side of Wareham Street, first about 1850 with a home for his son, John S. Benson, and later with house lots

The east side of Spruce Street continued to be developed through the early 1900s, at which time the Frederick E. Braley House was built. Braley was an anomaly among South Middleborough residents, being one of the few to find an occupation outside the lumber industry. Braley worked as a shoe cutter, engaged in the industry at Middleborough. The Braleys sold the house in 1926.

for John Witham (circa 1862), Abiel N. Fuller (1871) and Edwin F. Witham (1877). Adjoining Benson's property on the east was the Reed Farm at Wareham and Pine Streets, which saw development at this time with houses for teamster Roswell D. Houdlett (circa 1882) and Philander Southworth.

With the introduction of interurban street railway service in 1901, South Middleborough would become more accessible, and residents there could conceivably consider commuting to work in Middleborough center, thereby making it ripe for residential development. Potential property developers, however, found themselves stymied by South Middleborough's tradition of land consolidation and landholding. In April 1908, the *Gazette* unfairly sniped:

> *We hear of parties who would like to buy land in this locality and put up nice houses, but those who have land to sell want it covered with money. Still, if they were taxed one quarter what they prize it when asked to sell they would be on their high heels in a hurry. It used to be said it was a poor rule that wouldn't work both ways, but there are many of them nowadays.*

Clearly, the *Gazette* never recognized that the agricultural basis and traditional anti-tax bias of the community were deeply rooted. In a community where, by tradition, the land provided the livelihood for its residents, a natural disinclination arose to parting with property, as doing so could conceivably compromise the ability to provide economically for family members. Older South Middleborough residents no doubt recalled from parents or grandparents that lack of sufficient land had been the cause of the most severe controversy in the history of the local church a century before. Land at South Middleborough was not considered by its residents to be idle property to be covered with houses but as potentially income-producing agricultural land, the value of which lay in the large size of the parcels. All this being said however, this conception of land and its role would be radically altered following 1900, with the decline of the agricultural basis of the community economy and the arrival of a new invention: the automobile.

4

THE AUTOMOBILE ARRIVES, 1902–1924

Ten years ago the idea of sitting in a rapidly moving and handsomely equipped electrical car and meeting your friend steaming along in his automobile as you boomed down the pike from South Middleboro and Rock would have been scouted as an absurd proposition.
—Middleboro Gazette, *1901*

Just as a revolutionary transportation advance had inaugurated a new historical era in South Middleborough with the arrival of the railroad in 1848, so too would the appearance of the automobile in South Middleborough in the first decades of the twentieth century herald a new period of economic growth, one founded on the automobile and the passing tourist and one that would rouse the community from the economic malaise into which it had slipped following the decline of its lumber industry after 1910. Though the appearance of the automobile would bring an end to the agriculturally based economy of the community, it would also usher in new opportunity. Ironically, the instrument that was to prove to many the economic salvation of South Middleborough was initially regarded as an unwelcome intrusion into the peacefulness of the community. The automobile was considered annoying, with its perpetual clouds of lingering dust, and dangerous, jeopardizing the safety and lives of South Middleborough residents. Near-weekly diatribes against reckless and inconsiderate motorists became a common feature of local news reporting. The routing of State Route 28 (initially one of only two through routes linking Boston with the summer resorts of Cape Cod) through the historic heart of the village at South Middleborough ensured a heavy volume of traffic, with the consequent accidents and fatalities.

MIDDLEBORO, WAREHAM & BUZZARDS BAY STREET RAILWAY

While the improvement of South Middleborough's roadways following 1900 would ultimately have the unintended result of fostering improved communication between South Middleborough and its neighboring communities and fostering the growth of the automobile, the true harbinger of better transportation links was believed, at the time, to have been the Middleboro, Wareham & Buzzards Bay (MW&BB) Street Railway, which operated an electric trolley line through South Middleborough between 1901 and 1924. The street railway eventually would become an integral part of the community, serving the function formally performed by the steam railroad, providing the community with a critical transportation link for its residents and businesses to the world beyond South Middleborough.

Construction of the line began in March 1901 with the receipt in Middleborough of "several" carloads of rails and sleepers that were carted by Charles H. Thomas to various points along the proposed route between Middleborough center and Rock Village. During the fourth week of May 1901, additional carloads of rails were received at Middleborough, Rock and South Middleborough stations. The rails, shipped directly from mills in Pittsburgh, Pennsylvania, weighed some fourteen hundred pounds each, and a total of fifteen hundred tons would ultimately be required for the entire project. Additionally, more of the sixty thousand sleepers required were received from Hurd & Co. of Boston and were distributed as far as South Middleborough.

The contract for the construction of the line was awarded to Thomas & Connor of Middleborough in April 1901, and work began the next month when forty workmen broke ground at Barden Hill in Middleborough. By July 3, the line had reached the Rock station, a distance of about five miles. Cars tested on the completed stretch of line later that month made the run from Middleborough to Rock in just fifteen and a half minutes, and that portion of the line was opened for public use by August. During the summer

The Lyman P. Thomas House was constructed in 1906–07 on the site of the earlier 1776 Thomas house by South Middleborough's leading resident of the day. Thomas (1861–1929) was an engineer and contractor by profession whose projects included the Middleboro, Wareham & Buzzards Bay Street Railway. Later a partner in Thomas Brothers' store at South Middleborough, Thomas held numerous elected political positions locally, including Plymouth County commissioner.

of 1901, construction progressed at the rate of about half a mile per day, with poles to carry the heavy electrical feed wire being rapidly set; by early August, the line had finally reached South Middleborough.

Though the line would attempt, somewhat in vain, to promote its passenger service (in the spring of 1903, the sign "Mayflowers in Bloom—Take this Car" was seen on the MW&BB cars), the line passed through a sparsely populated region for a considerable extent and would be more significant for South Middleborough as a carrier of freight rather than people. The line did, however, permit local residents in South Middleborough to commute more easily to manufacturing or retail jobs at Middleborough center, thereby expanding the limited economic opportunities that had been previously available. Nonetheless, ridership remained small, and the street railway consequently devoted much effort to developing the freight portion of its business. At South Middleborough, John L. Benson & Company made regular use of the MW&BB freight service, shipping logs on the railway and even contemplating the construction of a spur to the Benson mill in 1906 (it was never built). Cranberries were also shipped by the street railway in such quantity that the drop in shipments of the fruit over the road during the 1905 season was believed to have been a considerable financial blow for the company.

The introduction of so novel a form of transport was initially fraught with a number of accidents, as residents were seemingly—and tragically—oblivious to the potential dangers the trolley cars posed. In the summer of 1902, Miss Tirzah Morse was struck by a car on the line in South Middleborough and "severely shaken and bruised" while apparently walking directly on the tracks. This incident may have prompted another similar occurrence just a month later when Michael Howard, who had recently located to South Middleborough, was killed by an MW&BB trolley car in a "case appearing like one of deliberate suicide. He ran from a house toward the car as though to hail it, and plunged forward to the track as it approached. He was instantly killed, the wheels passing diagonally over his head, and crushing it badly."

Howard's death appears to have been the single fatality on the line in South Middleborough, though periodic accidents there would continue to occur. In December 1905, Clarence H. Wilbur attempted to cross the track in front of an oncoming trolley car, "and the result was a collision and his wagon much the worse for the encounter."

ROAD IMPROVEMENTS

Concurrent with the construction of the Middleboro, Wareham & Buzzards Bay Street Railway through South Middleborough was the improvement of South Middleborough's roadways, which would literally pave the way for the future economic development of the community and its transformation from an agriculturally based economy to one centered on the provision of services to passing motorists. Not surprisingly, road improvements in South Middleborough were undertaken at the turn of the century not to encourage the automobile but rather to aid the local lumber industry. The object of improving local roads was one shared by most South Middleborough residents, as it was believed that it would facilitate the teaming of lumber to the local mills, and the community long advocated such improvements. As late as 1922, the local correspondent for the *Middleboro Gazette* remarked that "much improvement has been made on the country roads in this vicinity, but there is room for more."

Ironically, it was the lumber teamers, themselves, who were largely responsible for the sorry condition of local roadways. In 1897, after rebuilding the first section of the State Highway at Fall Brook in Middleborough, the State Highway Commission had to instruct teamers to drive in the middle of the road, "but as long as drivers think that the road is too hard for their horses feet it is probable that they will continue to use the side of the road." The following year, the state required that teamers change from narrow to wide wheels on their wagons to minimize damage to roadways; "that it will be conducive to better roads is generally conceded."

Among the earliest road improvements of the period in South Middleborough was the reconstruction of Pine Street, supported widely by the community in early 1906 from the standpoint of economic opportunism. "The road passes through a country rich in timber land, and its improvement is especially desired in that it will open up a good road to get lumber to the mills." The road, by this time, had been greatly damaged by years of heavy teaming activity and was much in need of repair. Work was ordered

This view depicts what is now Spruce Street near its present-day junction with Wareham Street. When the photograph was taken about 1910, this constituted part of the main route to Cape Cod. As automobiles became more prevalent, motor traffic on the road increased greatly, a development for which neither the roadway nor the community was initially equipped. Speed, noise and dust all became common causes of complaint.

by the county commissioners—who, not coincidentally, included Lyman P. Thomas of South Middleborough—and was completed by December 1908.

By far, the most significant development regarding South Middleborough's roadways, and the one with the farthest-reaching impact, was the reconstruction of Wareham Street immediately following the turn of the century and its designation as a state road. This development would dramatically and irrevocably alter the course of South Middleborough's economic and historical development.

In 1897, the town opted to use its state highway appropriation of $3,000 "in continuing the road[work] on Wareham street towards the Cape." Three years later, the Plymouth County Commissioners issued a decree to straighten Wareham Street, which then ran in a large arc from present-day Rocky Gutter Street through the woods toward South Middleborough, necessitating the building of one and a half miles of new road: the straight portion of Wareham Street north of South Middleborough, which is still known to some as the "South Middleborough Stretch." Partially financed by the New England Telephone Company and the Middleboro, Wareham & Buzzards Bay Street Railway Company, both of which were granted franchises over the new roadway, the work was completed in 1902. In November 1904, the town would complete macadamizing Wareham Street from South Middleborough to Rochester.

Though the much-needed improvement in Wareham Street was a factor in encouraging its use as a main thoroughfare, it was its designation as a state road, ultimately known as Route 28, that would draw the traffic that would transform South Middleborough's economy. State roads were known to be in better repair than local roads and provided a more direct route to destinations, thereby attracting what little vehicular traffic there was at the time. As the number of automobiles grew during the first quarter of the twentieth century, however, so too did the traffic utilizing the state roads, including Wareham Street.

THE TRAFFIC MENACE

Though the improvement of local roads following 1900 was undertaken to facilitate local teaming activity and not to accommodate outside motorists, that was precisely the effect that the relocation and improvement of Wareham

Street had, attracting motorists bound for Cape Cod. Each year, the opening of the "auto season," which accompanied the arrival of warmer weather in mid-May, was a dreaded occurrence in South Middleborough (as indicated by the following news items from the *Middleboro Gazette*), bringing as it did reckless drivers speeding through the heart of the village.

> *Automobiles driven at high speed over the macadam road in this village have caused the residents to stand aghast, when they are not hiking for shelter behind stone fences so that they may not be picked up in sections. (1905)*

> *Autos have begun their work of killing whatever comes in their way, beginning on a dog owned by Robert McLeod, knocking the breath out of it quicker that it takes to tell it. (1906)*

> *The way some autos rush along our streets is terrible…trying to see how fast they can go, and very often no warning is sounded when they pass either teams or foot passengers. It is especially dangerous for children. (1908)*

> *If the people at* [Middleborough center] *think the autos are going recklessly through their streets they had better make a tarry in this locality for a week and see the speed shown. It is not safe surely for the children. (1909)*

> *Autos have commenced their season of fast driving, as well as racing. Not that all are guilty of both, but enough of it is seen to convince anyone that those are the points seeming to be striven for by a larger part. (1911)*

> *It was almost a continuous stream of autos Sunday from early in the morning til late at night, all passing along the street as if in a great hurry to get to their destination. (1914)*

Initially, local authorities seemed inert in the face of this unprecedented transportation revolution and the potential dangers it posed. The South Middleborough correspondent lamented the speed with which drivers raced through the village, "as if the drivers were mad with themselves and all the world," and thought "it strange that no one has interfered with them." Eventually, however, the town countered with a new response: speed traps. The speed trap became so relied upon at South Middleborough that a 1906 automobile journal that provided tips for motoring enthusiasts warned readers of South Middleborough, "Constables are taking the numbers of every auto that goes past with any speed." Neighborhood boys tried a slightly different approach that Independence Day, much to the consternation of speeders:

> *Many of the autoists traveling here the other day were annoyed by pranks of boys. An effigy of a policeman holding a flag on which were the words, "Hold Up"* [the signal for a speeding motorist to halt], *was placed at the spot where selectmen recently held up so many drivers for over speeding. Several who were running fast, seeing the supposed officer, came to a stop, and found nothing but a well-made "dummy."*

Speeding accounted for numerous accidents in the area, with motorists careening into James M. Clark's wall (1906), through Ephraim H. Gammons's front yard (1910) and even into Frank Short's cranberry bog (1910). The *Gazette* took perverse pleasure in regaling readers with the details of each accident, presumably providing a cautionary tale for such speed-inclined motorists. South Middleborough residents, however, were compassionate in caring for victims of such accidents, occurring literally on their doorsteps, and numerous accounts of residents taking in complete strangers, caring for and boarding them or transporting them for medical treatment at Middleborough center have been left on record.

Initially, while no South Middleborough residents were physically injured by the automobiles streaming rapidly through their village, early reports of frightened horses and the many family pets struck by passing motorists sadly abound. Numerous dogs were killed by careless motorists, and even in 1924, the local correspondent felt compelled to caution residents to "guard your pet cat as closely as possible."

Though safety was the overriding concern of South Middleborough residents relative to automobile traffic, they were also greatly annoyed by the "almost continual cloud of dust" motorists raised. This was, in part, remedied in June and July 1911, when Wareham Street was oiled and tarred. "All are rejoicing at the great improvement upon the street [though]…only those who live on Wareham Street know how to appreciate it." However, even the preparation of the road was not without incident. In late June, a Cotuit-bound motorcyclist collided with the street sweeper, confusing the dust of the road with smoke from a fire.

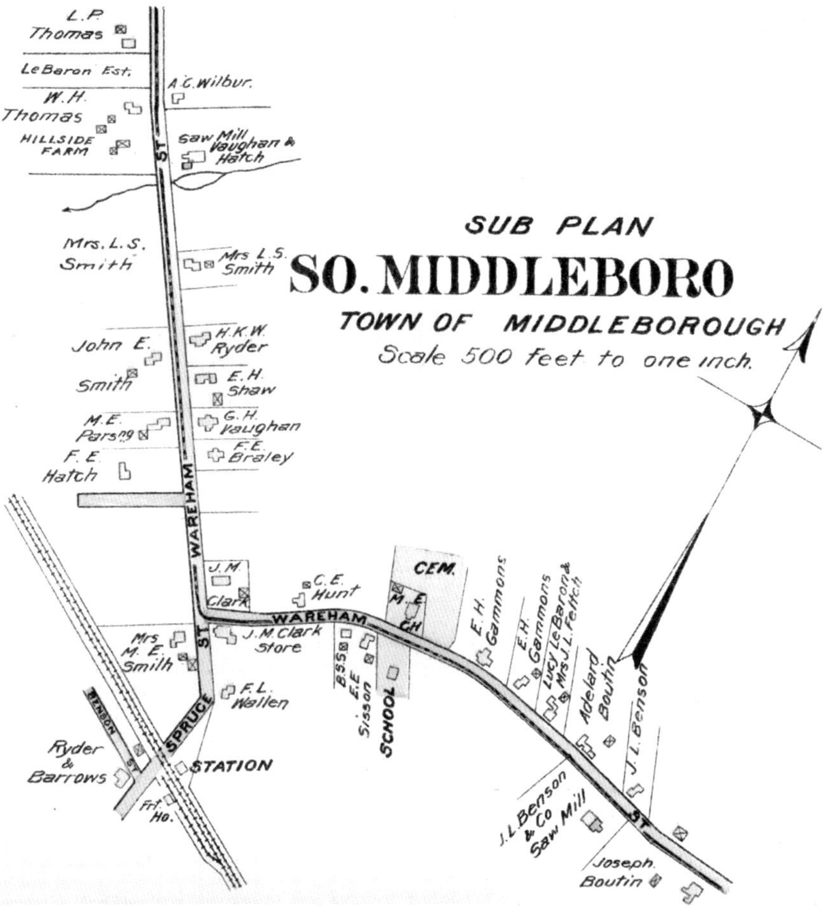

This 1903 map of South Middleborough shows the concentration of residences and institutions around Clark's Corner. The main route between Middleborough and Cape Cod passed through Clark's Corner, as did the Middleboro, Wareham & Buzzards Bay Street Railway, the path of which is marked by the heavy line. The street railway was immediately popular, and its arrival led to a further decline in passenger traffic on the older steam railroad.

Tragically, and inevitably, worse would come. The first South Middleborough auto fatality seems to have been elderly Harper Delano, who, on the evening of September 20, 1914, "when attempting to get out of the way of an auto…stepped directly into the path of another" near Clark's Corner. He died four nights later from his injuries. Delano's death touched off a firestorm of protest in South Middleborough, as for years the community had sought, without success, the construction of a sidewalk in the village.

MUNICIPAL SERVICES FOR A PERIPHERAL VILLAGE

Despite the transportation revolution that came to South Middleborough after 1900, the arrival of other means of communication and the provision of municipal services and amenities (including sidewalks) proved slow, a consequence of the community's peripheral position within the town of Middleborough as a whole. In this regard, South Middleborough was much like other small outlying villages throughout the region.

Telephonic communication did not arrive until 1907, when a "Farmers' Line" was completed in March of that year, nearly a quarter century after its introduction at Middleborough center, and electric street lighting was not provided until about 1913. Police protection, too, was late in coming and was not provided until 1909 in the form of a "special officer." Fortunately, crime in South Middleborough was for the most part not serious and was confined largely to petty thefts, though break-ins at South Middleborough's various stores had historically been high, including instances reported by Chandler R. Smith (1858) and James M. Clark (1871, 1875, 1880, 1906 and 1909). Robert McLeod, then serving as a clerk in Clark's store, was named the village's first special officer following a campaign by the South Middleborough correspondent of the *Middleboro Gazette*. McLeod's first arrest was made in July 1909. McLeod also served in this capacity to thwart potential motor vehicle violations. "Autoists may think that in this out-of-the-way place they can go without lights or do most any other unlawful things but it would be well for them to remember that we have a special officer here who has a sharp eye out for them and is not afraid to show his badge when occasion demands."

One of the longest struggles by the community centered on the construction of its sidewalks. For years, the neighborhood sought, without success, the construction of a sidewalk at Clark's Corner, and the matter became one of greater urgency with each passing season as the number of automobiles utilizing the streets mounted. "We are almost hopeful we are to have a sidewalk built, but the prospect looks more as though a gutter was to take the place of it as the road scraper has been over it and lowered instead of raising for a walk," commented an observer in 1911.

Though the lack of a sidewalk in South Middleborough may have appeared a minor cause of grievance to some, without a sidewalk residents were forced to walk in the streets; this became increasingly treacherous as

A view of Clark's Corner shortly after the turn of the last century, as seen from the southeast looking along Spruce Street toward the James M. Clark House at the center of the view and the South Middleborough store on the right. For a century and a half, Clark's Corner was the center of South Middleborough until the construction of a portion of modern-day Wareham Street bypassed it in 1925–26.

motor vehicle traffic along Wareham Street increased. Bicyclists, too, posed a problem for pedestrians, and locals advocated enforcement of the law requiring lights on bicycles, citing several narrow escapes from collisions with them while walking.

The 1914 death of Harper Delano only fueled the community's desire to have a sidewalk and underscored its contention that, without one, the neighborhood was unsafe for pedestrians. Finally, after years of hoping, South Middleborough saw its first modern sidewalk in the summer of 1916, when construction was begun in front of the South Middleborough church and was to progress in either direction until the full appropriation was expended. Nonetheless, there was a "wish that the town would have been more liberal" in terms of its appropriation and continuing dissatisfaction with the limited extent of the completed sidewalk coupled with unhappiness over the level of municipal services provided to the community.

Mild annoyance, however, once more turned to anger in 1919 following the tragic automobile-related death of another of the community's older residents, who was struck down in nearly the same spot as Harper Delano half a decade earlier. There was still no sidewalk at the spot. Following the

August 1919 death of Mrs. Drusilla Cartee, who was struck and killed by a passing truck near the parsonage on Spruce Street, the South Middleborough correspondent of the *Middleboro Gazette* lashed out, "Perhaps a few more occurrences like these will wake up the authorities."

It took another year however, before authorities were "awoken" and construction began on the sidewalk along the northeast side of Spruce Street stretching northward from Clark's Corner. Though residents were pleased with the proposed sidewalk, the project remained incomplete when, in August 1921, Mr. and Mrs. Ansel C. Wilbur were struck by an auto while returning home from Sunday evening services, prompting the *Gazette* to question, "A year ago a sidewalk was begun; why can't it be finished for the safety of the public?" The following month, an additional portion of the walk was constructed.

At this time, Reverend Robert E. Bisbee of Spruce Street sponsored the circulation of a petition for the completion of a sidewalk through the

Reverend Robert Bisbee (1858–1938) was photographed on Sunday morning, August 19, 1923, on his way to deliver a sermon as pastor of the South Middleborough church. Bisbee was a strong believer in the social imperative of Christianity and was well known for his *Essence of Christianity*, a brief pamphlet, the second edition of which he wrote at South Middleborough. *Courtesy of Middleborough Historical Association.*

village when Mrs. Lewis Bradshaw was struck by an automobile and her skull fractured while accompanying her husband to a Grange meeting. Miraculously, she survived, and her accident prompted the extension of the village's sidewalk northward to the house of Lyman P. Thomas and southward to that of Joseph Boutin. It was a hard price South Middleborough residents had paid, however, for the construction of but two miles of sidewalk.

Early Fire Protection

Another area in which South Middleborough was forced to fend for itself was fire protection. Fire was a constant threat at South Middleborough, not only to the village's homes and sawmills (which were especially prone to fire), but also to the great tracts of standing timber, a resource on which the prosperity of the community was founded.

South Middleborough's various sawmills, with their flammable wood-frame construction and contents, were particularly subject to the ever-present threat of fire, as demonstrated by fires in 1859, 1895, 1909 and 1915 that leveled, respectively, the mills of Benson & Smith, E.F. Witham, G.H. Vaughan and J.L. Benson. With their particular vulnerability, the local sawmills were the objects of especial vigilance by the community. Robert McLeod's first arrest following his appointment as a special (police) officer for South Middleborough was of a man discovered setting fires in the rear of Benson's mill in July 1909.

Woodland fires were also a frequent and serious threat to South Middleborough. The biggest culprit was the steam railroad, the locomotives of which produced drifting sparks capable of setting ablaze tinder-dry woodlands. Often fueled by a mix of slash and resinous pitch pines, these woodland fires could burn long and intensely hot, and the financial losses from such fires could prove staggering.

Locomotive-spawned fires tended to be seasonal, not appearing before Memorial Day, when the woods remained damp. Such fires became a common rite of summer, so much so that the *Gazette* adopted a somewhat blasé attitude toward their inevitable appearance and the threat they posed, reporting rather casually: "The first fire of the season to be set by the steam cars was on Monday [July 25, 1910] when three were set but a little way apart. The [railroad] section men attended to them and the downpour at night put them all out, which was fortunate." One of the earliest and most serious of these woodland fires in South Middleborough, however, occurred on April 28, 1855, when a fire burned over some sixty acres of woods, consuming in the process "quite an amount" of cut wood. The cause was supposed to have been a spark from a passing locomotive. "Fires have already begun by sparks from engines, one being set Wednesday noon." In May 1903, "locomotives caused two forest fires…one of them seriously threatening J.L. Benson's sawmill and only being stopped by over 100 men who worked energetically on the danger line." Two years later, railroad engines were responsible for fire on the lands of Lucinda Smith, John L. Benson, Fred Braley and the John Morse estate. "All were fortunate in a ready response from the people, who worked with a will to conquer them."

A more serious woodland blaze, on April 23, 1908, also started from sparks from a passing train on E.F. Witham's land and threatened Forest Hatch's house on (Old) Benson Street before local workmen and firefighters from Atwood's mill in Rock Village brought the fire under control. "The Hatch house was saved just in time," reported the *Middleboro Gazette.* A few days following this fire, a second one, also ignited by a passing locomotive, set fire to a portion of Frank L. Wallen's and John L. Benson's land near the depot. Yet another fire on October 4, 1910, again believed to have been set by a locomotive, "burned over quite a little woodland" near John L. Benson's mill field and Joseph Boutin's northeast of the depot. Despite it being the third fire reported in a short time, the *Gazette* stated that "fires thus far have not been as plenty as usual this season."

The railroads, because of the enormous liability, were keen to reduce the number of and damage from fires arising from their locomotives, particularly after 1909, when the commonwealth made them liable not only for any damages resulting from a locomotive-spawned fire but also for the costs incurred by communities in extinguishing such fires. Spark arrestors were adapted to engines and were ultimately required by state law. In the fall of 1913, the New York, New Haven & Hartford Railroad began to clear large swaths of land along its right of way on Cape Cod, farther down the line from South Middleborough. The railroad ultimately cleared some forty-five miles of line on the Cape and, in so doing, greatly reduced the number of fires the following year. Though there is no record of it, the practice was probably shortly thereafter adopted in South Middleborough, as indicated by the decline in the number of forest fires reported at that location in the local newspapers. Charles P. Rood, the fire claim agent for the New York, New Haven & Hartford, "told of the work accomplished by the railroad in clearing the side of the tracks from four to eight rods on each side" at a forest wardens' meeting in Middleborough in March 1916, further lending credence to the view that this practice was resorted to at South Middleborough following 1914.

Railroads, though common contributors to fires throughout the region, were not the only source. In late June 1858, a lightning strike set the woods ablaze just east of South Middleborough, destroying forty cords of cut wood belonging to Stillman Benson and burning several acres of standing timber belonging to Colonel Lothrop Thomas and others. In addition, house and barn fires occurred periodically. On the night of September 29, 1856, Marcus and Linus Bumpus lost their barn on Beach Street in a blaze they had little power to quell.

To combat these fires, South Middleborough relied on a community effort and often the goodwill of local workers, including the workforce of Atwood's mill in Rock. Eventually, Edward E. Sisson was named district fire warden for South Middleborough, and his resources in 1918 were listed as "five fire extinguishers, three belonging to the town of Middleboro, two belonging to the Grange, one extension ladder, loaned by the moth department, giving this district a good house fire protection as well as forest fire protection." The community was assured that "Mr. Sisson will always be at your service."

Despite this seeming lack of firefighting apparatus, South Middleborough, in fact, was the best-equipped district outside Middleborough center—in recognition of the devastating potential a fire in that area might have. Waterville and East Middleborough each were provided with only two extinguishers, while Rock, Fall Brook and Rocky Meadow each had only one.

The Decline of Lumbering

Clearly, as reflected in the debate over the provision of sidewalks and the area's early experience with fire protection, there existed a residual feeling within the South Middleborough community of being short-changed, a lingering resentment from the previous century. Certainly, the Town of Middleborough's seeming laxity in providing services to South Middleborough continued to stoke these feelings, which would find political expression in the formation of the Precinct Three Improvement Association two decades later. Even the length of time the town required to clear South Middleborough's roadways, as opposed to those at Middleborough center, following a snowstorm was considered a slight and, as such, open to criticism, in this instance by the *Middleboro Gazette*'s South Middleborough correspondent:

> *It does not seem just to this or any other part of the town to be so long delayed in having the roads cleared for travel after a snow...but of course if an accident should happen through delay we hope our town is fully able to meet all demands.*

Critics of South Middleborough charged that the village lacked interest in the welfare of the town as a whole and merely sought to benefit itself at the expense of the town.

Undoubtedly, South Middleborough's feelings of receiving the short end of the economic stick were exacerbated by the decline of the lumber industry. The period preceding World War I was one of transition for South Middleborough, noted for the decline of the lumber milling upon which the livelihood of the community had been based for two generations. A number of factors contributed to the decline of the lumber industry locally during this period. The rise of southern mills that processed yellow pine; the demise of the wooden box industry, which was replaced by the manufacture of paper boxes; the financial collapse of the Middleborough milling concern Clark & Cole, which left a string of bankruptcies in its wake; the local failure to adopt modern forestry practices; the accompanying failure to diversify in the face of a declining demand for white pine lumber and boxboards; the development of "portable" mills; and the devastation of large tracts of woodlands off Pine Street by the hurricane of 1944 all contributed to the decline of the once-dominant lumber industry in South Middleborough during the first decades of the twentieth century. When mills such as Vaughan's and Benson's were lost to fire (in 1909 and 1915, respectively), it seemed economically unprofitable to rebuild them, and the industry simply faded away. Hunt's mill at Houdlett's Corner survived until 1924 but was not rebuilt following its destruction by fire in that year due to an unpromising lumber market. Only the Fresh Meadows sawmill, operated by the Shurtleff family following 1945, survived. It, too, succumbed to fire in 1963.

Thomas Brothers' Store and the Narragansett Milling Company

Despite the decline of the local lumber industry after 1910 and the consequent economic downturn within the community, commerce as represented by the South Middleborough store thrived, and the operation modernized and expanded during this period. Earlier, in 1892, James M. Clark had relocated his store across Locust Street to the building where it remained a landmark for the next half century. As recalled by Jennie Gammons, the new store, like the old, served as a convenient and informal meeting place for the community. "Early morning customers discussed cattle purchases as they warmed themselves around the central heating stove, and phoned long distance to Boston when they wanted to check the market reports."

In November 1912, Clark sold the South Middleborough store to Robert McLeod, who had clerked for Clark since 1902. McLeod made immediate improvements. In February 1913, he erected a large barn to house the teams that drew the store's order wagons on F.L. Wallen's land nearby. Other

Though preceded by smaller stores such as Cobb's and Chandler R. Smith's, the South Middleborough store established by James M. Clark about 1863 would remain in operation until 1959. In 1892, the store relocated from the Clark House across Locust Street to this building. At the time this photograph was taken about 1914, the store was owned by Robert McLeod, who had formerly clerked in the store since 1902.

improvements included the electrification of the store in the late spring of 1913 and the purchase of a new horse in April 1913.

McLeod's Store continued to rely on the horse-drawn order wagons to deliver groceries throughout the area. The firm's wagons covered a number of routes, including Carver, Tremont in Wareham and Rock in Middleborough, and despite the quaint picture of the general store delivery wagon making its rounds, driving order wagons could prove challenging. At times, deliveries could not be made due to the poor condition of the roads, though the improvement of Wareham Street facilitated deliveries to areas like Tremont. Weather was also problematic. Clark lost a horse to pneumonia on the Rock route following an excessively cold day, while McLeod was overcome by the heat in July 1912 while delivering on the Carver route.

In 1915, McLeod retired from the business, at which time the store was purchased by brothers Alvin E., Alfred and Lyman P. Thomas. Alvin Thomas had been a clerk in the store for both Clark and McLeod and was noted for the long tenure of his service, having been employed there since 1879. The store subsequently became known as Thomas Brothers' Company, and under the guidance of the Thomases, the business was thoroughly modernized during the immediate postwar era. The firm relied solely on the horse-drawn order wagons until May 1919, when a truck was purchased for deliveries, driven by Ralph Tripp. A second truck was added in December 1919, handled by Ernest E. Thomas, and in February 1921, a new auto was acquired by the firm. (The company did, however, retain its horses, at least through August 1920, when the loss of one was reported.)

To supplement the goods available at Clark's, a number of area residents operated peddle carts. In November 1908, Will Bearse started what appears to have been a short-lived meat cart, while Mr. Keyes of West Wareham operated a fish business with a route through South Middleborough from about 1874 through 1929.

The continued importance of agriculture within the community at this time prompted a new business development when, in 1920, Thomas Brothers' disposed of its grain business to the Narragansett Milling Company of Providence, Rhode Island. "Grain business became a burden, as the mechanical method of producing chicks outdid the mother hen and neighboring flocks were raised by the hundreds, instead of the dozen. So groceries and grain parted company," wrote Jennie Gammons. Joining Narragansett at the time the Thomas Brothers' grain business was sold

The Narragansett Milling Company, a Rhode Island–based feed store, established a branch at South Middleborough in 1920 when it purchased Thomas Brothers' grain business. Joining the company at the time as bookkeeper and office manager was Chester W. Thomas, a former clerk at Thomas Brothers', who was photographed sometime during the 1930s in the company of Ralph Tripp outside the Spruce Street store.

was Chester Thomas, a former clerk at Thomas Brothers', who would remain with Narragansett for seventeen years as a bookkeeper and office manager. In 1925, Narragansett leased a separate storehouse at the South Middleborough depot, where it received grain by the carload and where agricultural presentations were occasionally held. Narragansett continued to operate until November 30, 1937, when it closed its doors at South Middleborough for good.

Agriculture and the South Middleborough Grange

The operation of the Narragansett Milling Company store as a separate entity was indicative of the continuing presence of agriculture at South Middleborough. The early 1900s witnessed a boom in poultry raising, while the cultivation of potatoes became important as well. In 1895, Frank Short raised on an acre and a half of land some 280 bushels of potatoes, the bulk of which were destined for market. Potato cultivation received renewed impetus in the late 1910s largely due to the influence of Henry W. Casey, a former resident of Millinocket, Maine. In November 1917, Casey purchased "all the cleared land of J[ohn] L. Benson, including the big barn" on Wareham Street, with the intention of "farming on quite an extensive scale." The Casey farm seems to have been devoted nearly exclusively to potato cultivation, and though the *Gazette* was initially unable to calculate "the number of hundreds of bushels to be harvested" in 1918, it was later reported to be 1,150. Casey, however, died that same summer, and the project of raising potatoes at South Middleborough on a grand scale was abandoned.

Helping foster agricultural development locally was the South Middleborough Grange, which was organized on December 6, 1913, with twenty-nine charter members and Master Lyman P. Thomas. The organization's avowed goal was "to foster better prospects in the field of agriculture and social opportunities for all, regardless of race, creed or politics," and it proved immediately popular. Its ranks grew steadily and reached eighty members by early January 1914, when a Grange hall on the second floor of Benson's sawmill was unofficially inaugurated. Dues for

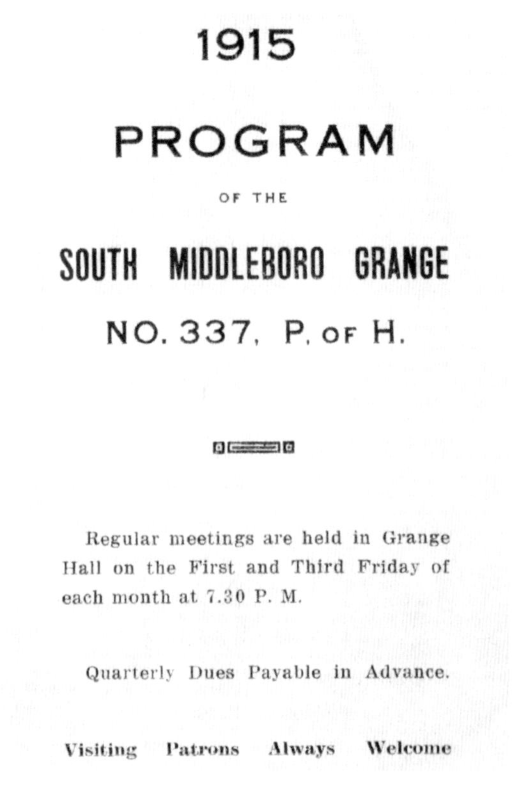

1915

PROGRAM

OF THE

SOUTH MIDDLEBORO GRANGE

NO. 337, P. OF H.

Regular meetings are held in Grange Hall on the First and Third Friday of each month at 7.30 P. M.

Quarterly Dues Payable in Advance.

Visiting Patrons Always Welcome

Formation of the local Patrons of Husbandry was recorded in the *Middleboro Gazette*: "The organization of a Grange here is attracting much interest. Last Wednesday evening a meeting in interest of the movement was held at the church, with about 20 prospective members and others present." Since its establishment in 1913, the South Middleborough Grange has been a prominent contributor to the social life of the South Middleborough community.

membership in the Grange were established at fifteen cents a month for ladies and twenty cents for men.

Throughout 1914 and 1915, the hall at Benson's mill was used for official Grange business, as well as farm discussions, debates, spelling bees, readings, musical programs, children's events, entertainments, socials and dancing. According to the *Middleboro Gazette*:

> *The young people who are interested in learning to dance gather at Grange hall one or more nights each week and are given instructions by some members who are not new to the work. One young miss was so excited, after taking some lessons, that she got a younger sister out of bed in the night and tried to get her to dance with her, but she preferred to sleep rather than to dance at that unheard of hour.*

On the night of December 7, 1915, the Grange hall was destroyed when the Benson mill was leveled by a fire believed to have originated in the mill's boiler room. "The mill was so far gone when the fire was first seen that it was useless to try and save anything, and the attention of the neighbors was directed to preventing the flames from catching on the roof of Joseph Boutin's stable." Following its loss, the Grange found temporary quarters in the church vestry, as well as the local schoolhouse, though according to Bernice Thomas, "several buxom members found the seats not to their fancy" in the latter location.

In 1916, the Grange erected its own hall on land acquired for $100 on Wareham Street near the schoolhouse and church. Lyman P. Thomas, Edward E. Sisson and Josiah Vaughan were named a committee to plan for the erection of the hall at a cost of $2,900. Members were asked to contribute. William H. Thomas generously donated pine logs for the project; these were milled into boards by Grange members. The hall was built by local builder Clarence Ryder and was in informal use as early as August 1, when a meeting was held in the unfinished building and a vote taken to purchase twelve settees from the Rock Church at one dollar each. In November, "inspection of the local grange was held…in their new hall, which is now nearing completion. A nice lunch was served and it was pronounced a very enjoyable evening." The hall, as completed, consisted of a basement kitchen and banquet hall, with a large hall and stage on the upper floor.

Founded to promote agriculture and better social opportunities for the community it served, the South Middleborough Grange enjoyed its greatest

Following the destruction of its hall, which was located on the second floor of John L. Benson's sawmill, in December 1915, the local Grange constructed its own building. Construction of the Craftsman-style South Middleborough Grange Hall was a community effort, with members contributing however they could. The hall, which is depicted shortly after its completion about 1916, remains in active use and is a prominent landmark in South Middleborough.

impact fostering its second goal. The Grange became well noted for several traditional functions, including its annual Labor Day clambakes, children's Halloween parties, December Community Christmas trees, whist parties and agricultural fairs, in addition to frequent lectures, plays, dances and pageants. The first clambake was held in 1917, and it became an important annual event. That same year, the first Grange fair was held on September 17, 1917, with a profit of sixty-four dollars. "Several years when traffic was heavy on Route 28, the Grange fairs were held at South Middleboro Fire Station." To this day, the South Middleborough Grange remains an active organization within the South Middleborough community.

SOCIAL CHANGE, WORLD WAR I AND POSTWAR IMPROVEMENTS

At the time that the formation of the South Middleborough Grange brought hitherto unprecedented social opportunities to the community, the community was undergoing a fairly substantial and dramatic social change.

The period between 1910 and 1925, in fact, would mark the greatest changes the community had seen since the arrival of the railroad in 1848.

World War I highlighted the community spirit of South Middleborough as residents did what they could for the war effort. Women engaged in knitting and Red Cross work, while young men like Theo Bearse enlisted for service in the army. Rationing was borne stoically, with the scarcity of sugar being perhaps the most difficult to endure. In 1917, it was remarked that the "lack of sugar is still the cry and there is great rejoicing when the promise of a pound is granted from the various grocers, and they are likewise very happy to be able to fill the order." More serious was the influenza pandemic, which made itself felt in South Middleborough in October 1918. South Middleborough was reported as "a very diseased little village," where proper nursing care was difficult to obtain, and the school was closed to prevent further spread of the disease. Though conditions had improved enough by October 20 that the ban on public gatherings was lifted, the seriousness of the flu was brought home with the death of Isaac Griffen, the son of Mrs. Charles Tripp of South Middleborough, who died of the disease while serving in the army at Camp Devens. He was South Middleborough's sole casualty of World War I.

With the announcement of the Armistice in November 1918, spontaneous celebrations erupted in South Middleborough. "Monday morning, when the news arrived of the 'peace' movement," reported the *Middleboro Gazette*, "the school was dismissed and the children, many of them, spent the rest of the day marching with horns, bells and drums, making all the demonstration possible, and they rung the church bell at various intervals."

Though the war itself did not bring great changes to South Middleborough, the flood of consumerism following it did. The immediate post–World War I era was one of rapid and dramatic technological and social change for South Middleborough, which witnessed the general introduction of electricity, indoor plumbing, telephones and radios into many homes and the acquisition of automobiles by many residents. In these respects, the community had lagged behind Middleborough center. Most South Middleborough homes were not wired for electricity until the First World War or after, with the houses of Edward E. Sisson (1916); Alvin E. Thomas, Ansel C. Wilbur and Lyman P. Thomas (1919); Lottie Feltch (1920); and Roswell Houdlett (1923) being the first to be electrified. The South Middleborough School was not electrified until 1922, and the parsonage, not until 1925. Despite this

Among the hobbies pursued by Herbert L. Wilber, the one that left the most lasting impression on South Middleborough was his masonry work. Numerous projects were constructed by Wilber from readily available fieldstone, including cellar foundations, chimneys, outdoor fireplaces and stone walls. Most ambitious of all was his own home (photographed in 1937), which he began in 1921 and which still stands on Wareham Street. *Courtesy of Middleborough Historical Association.*

advance, the early electrical service in South Middleborough often proved capricious, being susceptible to interruptions and failures. Indoor plumbing was another welcome innovation introduced during this period to South Middleborough, where it was installed in the homes of Lyman P. Thomas (1920), Oscar Mostrom (1920), Edward E. Sisson (1922), Ansel C. Wilbur (1924) and the Methodist Parsonage (1929).

Besides these changes, demographic developments were altering the community as well. South Middleborough had remained a relatively culturally homogenous community long after immigrants attracted by the prospect of industrial employment had begun settling elsewhere in Middleborough. The early twentieth century, however, brought the arrival of immigrants drawn to employment on the cranberry bogs in and around South Middleborough. A large number of Finns settled along France, East and Beach Streets and in adjacent South Carver and West Wareham, where they established a culturally distinctive and vibrant community and where many would later own cranberry bogs themselves. The first Finnish families to purchase property in South Middleborough were those of Kalle H. Liukko and O. Einar Kumpenen in 1915. Later families would include the Heleens (Helíns), Ericksons, Kaskis, Neimis, Timonens, Korhonens and Kustis along Beach Street and the Halunens, Lehtos, Korpinens and Pakkonens on France Street. The local Finnish population grew from six families in 1920 to eleven by 1930, many of them with younger children. During the early 1920s, fully one-third of the children attending classes at the South Middleborough School were Finnish American.

A second, smaller immigrant group adding to the growing diversity of South Middleborough during this period was the Cape Verdeans, a number of whom settled on Wareham Street midway between South Middleborough and Rochester. Like the Finns, the Cape Verdeans found work on the local cranberry bogs, and they, too, eventually rose to become bog owners. Notable among the early Cape Verdeans at South Middleborough were the Pina, Mendes, Ferreira, Rezendes, Fernandes and Barboza families.

5

THE TOURIST-BASED ECONOMY, 1924–1966

From the 20s to the present day [1961], *millions of motorists have passed through South Middleboro on busy Route 28 and remembered it, if they gave it a second thought, as a typical wayside collection of restaurants, gift shops and gas stations.*
—Middleboro Gazette, *1961*

The 1920s proved to be the watershed for South Middleborough's subsequent economic growth, all powered by the automobile. As Jennie Gammons trenchantly observed of South Middleborough:

> *A new era began with the auto. The sandy, village road was remade with macadam surface to become a part of Route 28 from Boston to the Cape. Gasoline service stations sprang up like plants from thickly sown seed. Old houses were sought for transformation into restaurants or for guests. Householders tidied up their property and set out climbing vines to cheer up the landscape. Signs, illuminated at night, dangled conspicuously to call in the tourist. The quiet, easy-going neighborhood awoke to find itself on a highway with commercial prospects.*

The community's initial aversion to the automobile underwent a dramatic reversal during the 1920s when the community began to recognize economic opportunity in the increasing number of motorists passing through the village, and new residents moved in to take advantage of the opportunities

Late for church, an unidentified parishioner hurries to services at the South Middleborough church on August 30, 1942. To the left side of the church can be seen the Scout Cabin. The juxtaposition of church and automobile reflects the changing circumstances of South Middleborough at this time as it moved from a community once spiritually centered on the church to one economically centered on the automobile. *Courtesy of Middleborough Historical Association.*

thus presented. Following 1924, numerous auto-related businesses, catering to tourists bound for or returning from Cape Cod, sprang up in South Middleborough, including filling stations, tearooms, restaurants, tourist camps, overnight cabins, motels and gift shops, stamping the community for the next forty years with a commercial vitality it had never before known.

EVOLVING TRANSPORTATION AND A NEW ROAD

Contributing to the local rise of the automobile was the decline of both the steam and street railway, and the somewhat erratic service of the bus lines that replaced them, an outcome that encouraged further use of the automobile. When in April 1917, the *Middleboro Gazette* reported two additional automobiles being acquired by South Middleborough owners and remarked, "Well, of course, the more the better," it signaled a newly receptive attitude toward automotive transportation not held in South Middleborough before the war. Yet despite this new expression of acceptance, the community, as a whole, remained dependent on the street railway.

Despite the initial skepticism with which South Middleborough residents initially greeted automobiles, the transportation innovation was soon accepted by the community, which recognized both its utility as well as the prosperity it brought in its wake. One early automobile owner at South Middleborough was Herbert L. Wilber, whose self-described "flivver" was captured in this photograph in May 1929. *Courtesy of Middleborough Historical Association.*

Throughout its brief lifetime, the street railway was appreciated as a vital link between South Middleborough and the larger world beyond, and in 1918 it was labeled "such a handy means of conveyance." Though rumored shutdowns of service failed to materialize, storm-related interruptions during the first months of 1920 led residents to ruminate about the potential impact of any permanent disruption. "The absence of the electrics on our street makes it very lonely, and if they were off for good it would make it most dismal." Throughout the later years of its existence, the street railway was plagued by stubbornly persistent rumors of a permanent cessation of operations, and such talk circulated for some time prior to the final abandonment in the early 1920s of the streetcar service, which was "driven out of business, local folks say, by a larger competitor…raising the price of electricity." The street railway was replaced by jitneys, a service that, itself, was discontinued in the spring of 1924 and was succeeded by buses. Bus lines arose locally in response to both the demise of street railways and the declining ridership on the area's railroads, as railroad companies began to curtail their passenger services. Throughout the decade following World War I, South Middleborough was under constant threat of losing its steam rail service, a service that became all the more vital following the demise of the street railway in 1923–24.

Meanwhile, automobile traffic passing through South Middleborough increased exponentially, prompting another road improvement scheme that would lead to the bypassing of Clark's Corner, the one-time heart of the community at the intersection of present-day Spruce and Locust Streets. While not a significant deterrent to traffic in a quieter age, the corner became increasingly notorious for motor accidents once Wareham Street was designated a state route and all Cape traffic was forced to take the sharp turn in the center of the village. "People do not seem to remember that there is such a corner, but find it out when rushing recklessly around it," wrote the *Gazette* correspondent somewhat unsympathetically in 1918. Nonetheless, to help minimize the number of accidents, in 1921 work commenced on widening the streets at the intersection. Pear trees on the Clark property

Photographed in 1935 just north of its intersection with Spruce Street, a broad and macadamized Wareham Street clearly invited motor traffic, as did the 1925 bypass of Clark's Corner visible to the left. Though facilitating through traffic to the Cape, by the early 1930s, the roadway was clogged each summer with weekend traffic. The two people stand near the Ansel C. Wilbur House. *Courtesy of Middleborough Historical Association.*

were, in Jennie Gammons's words, "transplanted to perish in another place," while the wall skirting the corner was moved back in January by Peter Johnson, and work was undertaken to widen the road in May and June. As if to demonstrate that the width of the roadway at the intersection was immaterial, an accident occurred there on July 23, 1921, just weeks after completion of the project.

Ultimately, because of the dangerousness of the roadway's configuration and the fact that Clark's Corner remained a popular area where locals walked (either to Thomas Brothers' or to the South Middleborough depot), a decision was made to circumvent the corner altogether through the construction of a new road or bypass. Work on the new roadway running from Wareham Street near the former Witham sawmill site southeastward to a point in front of the South Middleborough Church commenced in September 1925 and was completed in 1926, when its inauguration was ironically marred on opening day as it became the scene of four accidents, all attributed to speed. By July, the entire new roadway (along which the state highway was rerouted) was opened. The bypass was notable for a number of reasons, including the facilitation of through traffic to the Cape and the reduction of accidents at Clark's Corner. More significantly, by rerouting traffic away from Clark's Corner and opening new land for commercial development, the bypass prompted the relocation of South Middleborough's commercial activity to the opposite end of Locust Street. By 1948, Clark's Corner would be completely abandoned.

What laid the foundation for the successful transition of South Middleborough's economy was the volume of traffic that utilized the new road. While South Middleborough itself failed to become a destination location, it was able to cater to those tourists passing through the area en route to resorts on Cape Cod. Numerous guidebooks at the time directed toward the new motoring public declared the area of South Middleborough inconsequential from a sightseer's perspective. "From Middleboro to Wareham the State Road…runs through a rather flat and monotonous country interspersed with farms and tracts of scrub oak and pine." Similarly, the 1937 WPA guide for Massachusetts describes the route as passing "through open stretches of uninteresting country, with occasional thick pine groves to a junction with US 6" in Wareham.

Though uninteresting as it may have been from a motorist's point of view, Route 28 to Cape Cod opened South Middleborough to a sudden influx

Looking northward along Route 28 from in front of the home of Herbert L. Wilber, it can clearly be understood why the arrow-straight roadway became known as both the "South Middleborough Stretch" and the "straight stretch." Across the street is the Wareham Street Garage, established in the 1930s and operated by Henry P. Guerin. The two signs advertise Tydol-brand gasoline. *Courtesy of Middleborough Historical Association.*

of automobile traffic. So great was the volume of traffic (particularly on summer weekends and holidays) that the state employed William Wilcox of South Middleborough to count automobiles on the road as they passed. Traffic had become so heavy on the road by 1957 that *Gazette* editor Lorenzo Wood remarked that "were Willie to attempt the car counting task this summer, even on a day in midweek, we fear he would soon become the victim of St. Vitus dance, or some equally dreaded nervous malady before the clock struck high noon."

GASOLINE

South Middleborough benefited greatly from the postwar boom in automobile ownership and the subsequent growth of motor tourist–related services, the now clichéd trio of gas, food and lodging. During the period between the wars, the number of tourists bound for Cape Cod increased dramatically, with the majority of them conveyed there by automobile rather than by the steam train as formerly. To cater to these thousands of motorists, filling stations naturally abounded along the route.

The earliest appears to have been Sisson's, established in 1917 by Elmer A. Sisson on Locust Street in front of his father's blacksmith shop. The opening of the 1925–26 bypass forced Sisson to relocate his filling station and garage across the road. The new location was prominent at the junction of Locust and Wareham Streets, and his filling station, with its large sign on the roof advertising both automotive services and the diner across the roadway, could be seen for a considerable distance by motorists traveling north on Route 28. Sisson employed a number of local residents at the station, including Lewis Bradshaw, A. Tremaine Smith, Maurice Goodell and Arthur Carr. Though retail gasoline sales remained the operation's mainstay, by 1950 Sisson had branched into the fuel oil and bottled gas business, selling gas ranges and appliances as part of the operation, which was managed by Bill Greely, with employees Ed Tomasik and Ed Bemis. Sisson served Middleborough, Carver, Rochester and Lakeville with two oil trucks and one gas truck, all of which were housed in the old garage on Locust Street.

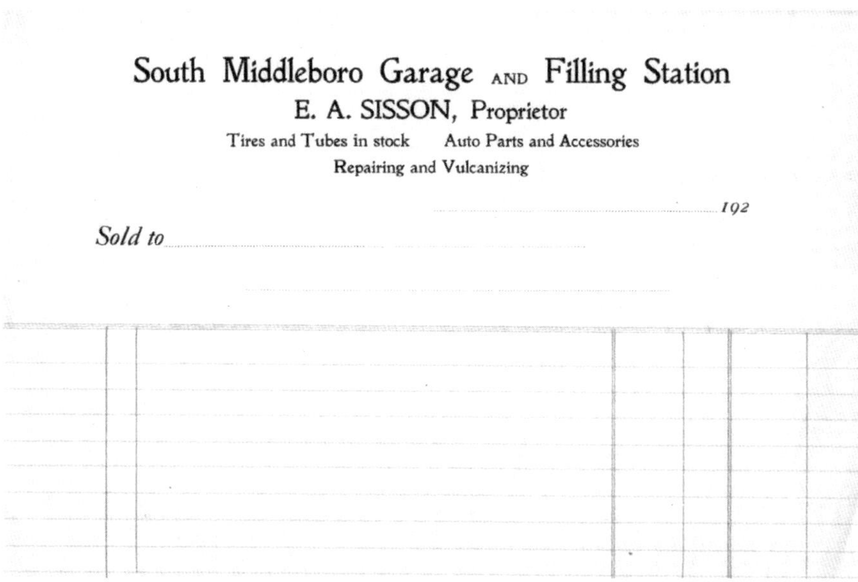
South Middleboro Garage AND Filling Station
E. A. SISSON, Proprietor
Tires and Tubes in stock   Auto Parts and Accessories
Repairing and Vulcanizing
192
Sold to

While the construction of a new stretch of Wareham Street in 1924–25 bypassing Clark's Corner eliminated the treacherous turn motorists had previously been required to make, it also opened additional land for commercial development. At this time, Elmer Sisson relocated his garage across Locust Street and constructed a new filling station and commodious three-bay service garage on one side of the bypass, establishing Sisson's Diner on the opposite side.

At the opposite end of the 1926 bypass, a second triangular-shaped lot of land at the intersection of Wareham and Spruce Streets less than a mile north of Sisson's had been created, and this too was considered ideally suited for the location of a filling station. In 1926, the Colonial Esso Gasoline Station was built at the northern end of the village by Clifford H. Barker of Allston and Walter H. Lennon of Arlington Heights, who recognized in it a prime retail location. Barker and Lennon operated the filling station through the close of the 1927 tourist season, at which time they sold the property to Frank A. Cavicchi of Arlington Heights, who would operate the station through 1944.

Initially, Cavicchi proposed operating the station throughout the year, but in December 1928, he closed for the winter, and the station would continue to operate only seasonally for several years, opening each April and shutting for the winter in November. On January 10, 1944, Cavicchi sold the station to Ralph G. Wilber of South Middleborough, who expanded the operation, installing larger underground tanks in 1946. Although Wilber sold the station on June 19, 1951, to the Southeastern Massachusetts Oil Corporation of Taunton, the station for many years remained informally known as Wilber's Filling Station. Owners

In early 1944, Ralph G. Wilber was photographed in front of the Colonial Esso filling station at the junction of Wareham and Spruce Streets. Wilber purchased the station in January 1944 and owned it until 1951. The photograph reveals the rather informal nature of South Middleborough's filling stations at the time. A small sign beside the telephone pole marks the road as Route 28. *Courtesy of Middleborough Historical Association.*

subsequent to Southeastern included the Esso Standard Oil Corporation (later Exxon) and, after 1979, Henry Tinkham.

A third filling station was located at Houdlett's Corner and appears to have been first operated by Margaret E. Cuddyer of Providence, who operated a wayside stand there that also sold gasoline. Cuddyer conducted the business as a seasonal operation, closing in December 1930, during the first year. She was succeeded by Frank B. Lewis, who came to South Middleborough and acquired the business in the early 1930s, operating it for fifteen years until 1947, when it was sold. Following Lewis's ownership, the station had a succession of owners.

While Sisson's, Wilber's and Lewis's stations were the largest and longest-lived gasoline retailers, many other small South Middleborough businesses retailed gasoline at one time or another, the sale of which was not as rigidly controlled as it is today. Recorded notices in the local newspaper indicate that small pumps stood in front of Donovan's, Shaw's, Osman Otis's, the White Arbor and the Old Stone House.

Food

In addition to gasoline, motorists driving to and from Cape Cod also sought clean, reputable restaurants and tearooms where they could stop for a quick and pleasant lunch. Among the most noted of these businesses established in South Middleborough was Sisson's Diner, which was created on the north side of the recently opened bypass across Wareham Street from Elmer A. Sisson's filling station.

Sisson is said to have remarked that he had established his diner here in 1926 because the corner "looked kind of bare." The remark was certainly self-deprecating, as Sisson was an astute businessman who keenly recognized the potential of the site located along the route to Cape Cod. To house the diner, in 1926 Sisson acquired a former trolley car from the defunct Middleboro, Wareham & Buzzards Bay Street Railway. The car selected had been in an accident, and as a consequence, one end was considerably smashed. The car was transported to South Middleborough by Harry Shurtleff by means of "a high-wheeled rig" designed for hauling logs from the woods. Once on-site, the damage to the car was repaired, and a tin ventilator was installed on the roof.

To operate the diner, Sisson engaged Harry Clark. Clark had previously operated what was believed to have been Middleborough's first diner and later conducted a restaurant in one of the local shoe manufactories. "It was fixtures in storage after the shoe factory restaurant was closed, which went into the converted trolley car." Clark was later assisted by his brother, William (Bill) L. Clark, and the two lived behind the diner for a time. Following 1948, the proprietor was Adrian Alberti. "Asked what were his credentials, one of the men [at the South Middleborough Fire Station in 1971] chuckled and replied—'He was a farmer.'" Lack of restaurant experience notwithstanding, Alberti conducted the diner business until September 1951, when he retired. It was Alberti's son, Alfred P. Alberti, or "Al," who became the better-known proprietor, taking charge of the diner following his return from service during World War II. The younger Alberti was remembered as "a man of great, good humor, with a greeting, and appropriate remarks for all comers. 'A lot of people came for the entertainment,' said one of his admirers." Though Sisson's remained a favorite with motorists passing through South Middleborough, locals, too, patronized the establishment. Particularly favored was "Fish Day" on Friday, when fish and fried clams would be served, attracting many of the men from the fire station across the road. Friday was the only day the diner stayed open past two o'clock in the afternoon, its regular closing hour.

Another early South Middleborough eating establishment popular with motorists was the White Arbor Tea Room, which operated in the former bungalow-style John L. Benson House, constructed in 1917 and presently owned by Coletti Brothers Oil Company. In 1922, Mrs. Mary A. Atherton of Dedham, Massachusetts, acquired the house for use as a summer home and named it White Arbor, but by 1927, it was being operated by Mrs. Atherton as a tearoom known as the White Arbor Tea Room, catering to Cape-bound motorists. In July 1928, under a new owner, Mrs. Gardner of Philadelphia, overnight accommodations were added, and the property was operated as the White Arbor Inn, which also sold gasoline to passing motorists. Following January 1934, the establishment was run by Mabel A. Brown, who seems to have been renamed it Briarwood, a likely reference to the woods that stood to the rear of the house and were undoubtedly filled (like much of South Middleborough's woods) with tangles of briars. It is unclear when Briarwood ceased to operate as a tearoom and inn, but the business appears to have become defunct sometime prior to World War II.

Similar in development from tearoom to inn was the Polly Pine Tea Room, which conducted business in what had once been a small soap manufactory situated on the southwest side of Wareham Street midway between Locust and Pine Streets. Begun as a light refreshment business following August 1925 by Miss Lillian C. White of Jamaica Plain, the Polly Pine later added accommodations for overnight guests and became known as the Polly Pine Inn. During the 1950 season, the Polly Pine operated four overnight cabins. It continued to operate as a restaurant through the 1968 tourist season.

Still farther south along Wareham Street were smaller refreshment operations, notable among which was that of Nicholas Leontos, who billed himself as "the Original Milk Shake King." In 1932, Leontos had acquired a parcel of land from William F. Shaw and established a business catering to Cape motorists, selling groceries, tobacco, toys, milkshakes and frappes.

Most extensive and upscale of all South Middleborough's eating establishments was the former Hell's Blazes Tavern on Wareham Street at the Rochester line; it was converted into a restaurant catering to tourists seeking a more leisurely and expansive meal. In March 1930, the main house, dating from

The Holmes family long owned the property known as Hell's Blazes. The last to do so, Salathiel Holmes, was said to have been so attached to the homestead that he never ventured farther than a few miles from it and only once in his lifetime slept under another roof. Four years after an elderly Holmes sold the property in 1926, it became a tearoom known as the Old Tavern.

about 1690; a cottage reconstructed from the barn; thirty acres of land; and thirty young apple trees were acquired by Edith M. Gates of Middleborough. During the summer of 1930, the property was opened as a tearoom and gift shop known as the Old Tavern and advertised luncheon, tea, lobster and chicken dinners. Noted guests of the establishment during its first season included Dr. Winthrop Adams, medical director of the U.S. Veterans' Bureau; Amos L. Taylor, chairman of the Massachusetts Republican Committee; and Frank J. Bunner, editor of the *Red Cross Courier*, the official publication of the American Red Cross. The property was sold in May 1935 by Mrs. Gates of Middleborough to Burton Davis of Arlington, who proposed operating the property as a tearoom. Financial difficulties seem to have plagued the proposal, however, and in September 1938, the Merchants Cooperative bank of Boston foreclosed on the property and retained the title until 1945, when it was sold to Basil K. and Martha E. Neftel of Middleborough.

Lodging

While many motorists traveling to Cape Cod today can make the journey in several hours, travel in the past might require an overnight stay en route, and accordingly a number of businesses providing overnight accommodation naturally arose along Route 28 in South Middleborough. The earliest lodgings tended to be what were known as overnight camps, followed by inns, small individual cabins and, finally, motels.

One of the first, if not the very first, facilities to provide lodging to Cape motorists in South Middleborough was the Capeway Tourist Camp of Harry F. and Elnora A. Vinton of Braintree. The camp was established along the north side of Wareham Street, midway between Houdlett's Corner and the Rochester line on the former Charles E. Tripp farm, which the Vintons purchased in March 1927 from Jule Ferreira with the intentions of opening a tourist camp and remodeling the old Tripp House on the property as a roadside inn. The venture was short-lived. The house was leveled by fire on August 15, 1927, and rather than rebuild, the Vintons sold the property. Similar in scope was the Old Stone House next to the South Middleborough Cemetery, which was equipped as an overnight camp as well. Here, motorists could find rudimentary lodging facilities, as well as gasoline. And, as noted previously, both the White Arbor and Polly Pine Inns also provided early accommodations for travelers through the district.

Lucy Braley's Candy Kitchen

In addition to providing services, South Middleborough entrepreneurs established numerous small-scale roadside stands to sell goods to passing motorists. Local produce, flowers and other items were sold at small wooden stands that were hastily erected following the First World War and operated seasonally, providing residents with a means to supplement their incomes. One of these businesses, Lucy Braley's Candy Kitchen, would become a popular local institution and a landmark for travelers bound for the Cape.

The business was conducted by Lucy (Braley) Sisson, wife of Elmer A. Sisson, who was originally a schoolteacher in Bridgewater but became a noted businesswoman in the area, known for her devotion to South Middleborough, as well as her "great perseverance." The business originated in Lucy Braley's affection for her niece Louise (Long) Tomasik when Lucy was in her twenties. Lucy Sisson explained in 1975, "She was my first niece and I loved her. I used to pick her up on weekends and we did things together—gardening and making candy…We sold flowers and vegetables at an improvised 'stand' on our lawn on Spruce Street." The pair decided

This 1930s view depicts the meticulously maintained Lucy Braley's Candy Kitchen, with expansive windows, cheerful canopy-striped awnings and window boxes, which beckoned travelers to and from Cape Cod with its inviting appearance. To the left is her husband's business, Sisson's Garage.

to try selling some of the candy they had made at the West Wareham home of Lucy's brother, Allen Braley, and found that "it was thrilling to take the money." The following summer, Lucy established a small candy shop at Elmer Sisson's filling station. Sisson, who was ill at the time, consented but requested that she assist Bill Greely in tending the station. "We made fudge in the back of the station," Lucy later recalled, "and were there for two summers." When a produce stand on property owned by Sisson next to the station went out of business, Lucy Braley was able to relocate there, though she claimed that the candy making "was still just a hobby" at the time.

Various innovative marketing techniques were employed by the business, resulting in its rapid growth. The Candy Kitchen maintained summer delivery routes in Onset, Wareham, Mattapoisett and Falmouth, with candy delivered by Ralph W. Wilbur and Bob Pope, who were also selling candy at various local beaches during the summer of 1938. Taking her cue from a practice once employed by the local ice industry, Lucy Braley requested that patrons residing at beach communities wishing to purchase candy place a pink card in their windows to indicate to the passing salesman that candy was wanted.

Over the years, the business employed more than one hundred people, largely local women, some of whom, as Lucy Braley was proud to note, were enabled to remain in school or pursue higher education due to their employment at the Candy Kitchen. "I can think of at least six who either went on to become teachers or influential persons." Among the employees were Helen R. Thomas, Mary Gurney, Harriet Welch, Marjorie Matthews, Helen Graham, Doris Smith and Ruth Freeman. "There are grown ups in the community whose education was materially advanced through the employment Lucy provided."

The candy produced at the shop itself was developed over time. Arthur Tripp, owner of Tripp's Candy Kitchen in Middleborough center, divulged his recipes for caramels, butter crunch and fudge sauce to Lucy Braley, who made the fudge sauce for Ben Howes' Chicken House, located at Wareham and Smith Streets just north of South Middleborough. Two of Lucy Braley's employees, Helen Graham and Doris Smith, attended courses in Boston, learning to make fondants (creamy centers), "and that's when our candy dipping began." The Candy Kitchen also shared its knowledge of candy making, giving a candy-making demonstration in November 1939 to the Eastern Star.

Interwar Recreation

While commercial enterprise during the interwar period expanded greatly, social life at South Middleborough during the same period continued as it long had. The Grange remained central to social activities in South Middleborough, while the local church played a lesser, though still noticeable role. Improved transportation connections with Middleborough made the center of town, with its movies, lectures and dances, an attractive alternative.

Social life in South Middleborough generally focused on communal activities, and further efforts were made in this direction in the 1930s with the establishment of a community tennis court constructed on land adjoining the Colonial Esso gasoline station during the summer of 1928 by Henrietta Wilbur, Annie Wilbur, Helen Thomas, Snowden Thomas, Robert Donovan and Henry B. Burkland. Later courts were located at Mrs. Lewis Bradshaw's

Tennis remained a popular pastime in the first half of the twentieth century, and a series of community courts were built to accommodate devotees of the sport, including Alden Wilbur (1901–1982), photographed here on July 12, 1916. "He happened to be dressed up," reads the caption, "because it was the day of the S[unday] S[chool] picnic and he had just got home." *Courtesy of Middleborough Historical Association.*

Hillside Farm and the Methodist parsonage on Spruce Street. The parsonage court was completed by August 1930, at which time the "young people" were reported as "deriving much pleasure from it." The following year, the first of a number of annual tournaments between South Middleborough and Rock residents were initiated, and in 1935, a South Middleborough Athletic Association was formed with the purpose of caring for the court. Though the association was reorganized in 1939, by the 1941 season, the Senior Epworth League of the church was preparing the court. Despite the several years of pleasure it gave South Middleborough residents, the community tennis court appears to have been abandoned during the Second World War.

Another community project was the rehabilitation of the so-called Scout House, which stood between Sisson's Diner and the Methodist Church. The Scout House had actually begun its life as a "discarded shed" owned by the South Middleborough Methodist Episcopal Church. In March 1938, the local Boy Scouts, with contributions from the Ladies' Aid Society and others, began reconstructing the shed for use as a meeting place, having previously met in the church vestry and the Grange hall. By late June, work on the cabin was nearing completion. Measuring a mere thirty-four by twenty feet, the rustic-style building would eventually become a small community center, hosting numerous local events and affairs, as well as providing a home for the South Middleborough Scouts and the South Middleborough branch of the Middleborough Public Library (1941–74). The Scout House often provided the venue for community functions during the mid-twentieth century when larger facilities such as the Grange hall or the Methodist Church vestry were unnecessary. During the 1950s square dancing fad, the cabin often hosted dances and lessons for young people and adults. Many of these dances were conducted for the benefit of the South Middleboro Protective Association and became an important social outlet for the community.

Perhaps, however, the most noted organization to have utilized the Scout House was the Middleborough Public Library, which established a branch in the building in 1941. South Middleborough had earlier had a branch library housed in the South Middleborough School. Opened to the public in October 1922, the library was supplemented with books generously contributed by community members. The *Middleboro Gazette* was a local vocal supporter of the South Middleborough branch library, the local correspondent reminding readers, "Do South Middleboro people realize and take advantage of their opportunity? Our branch library is waiting to serve you." Though

Augmenting both the Grange Hall and church vestry as community meeting places was the small Scout Cabin located between Sisson's Diner and the Methodist church. In the 1950s, the cabin was a common venue for square dances, which were highly popular and were sponsored at times (as seen here) for the benefit of South Middleborough's fire protection services.

the implication seems to be that residents failed to avail themselves of the branch library, such was not the case. In March 1924, some 106 books were in circulation from a collection that, in April 1924, totaled just 422 volumes. Through gifts and donations, local residents continued to support the branch library, which operated as late as 1928 but closed sometime thereafter.

In May 1940, the Precinct Three Improvement Association petitioned the Middleborough Public Library for the establishment of a branch at South Middleborough. Initially, there was some opposition to the request by voters residing outside South Middleborough who bridled at the admittedly minimal expense. "An old argument against a branch library here was the mistaken idea that it was not needed. In answer to request, it was stated 'Folks down there don't read.'" Later circulation figures belied that assertion, and by 1949, some 2,580 books were borrowed from the branch despite the fact that it was open only three hours weekly.

Shelves were installed in the cabin by James Graham to house the collection, and the branch library was opened on January 22, 1941, with hours from 1:00 to 9:00 p.m. each Wednesday. Town librarian Mertie E. Witbeck "furnished equipment, borrowers' cards, application blanks, a filing

One of the most anticipated events of the year was the church Sunday school picnic, held at various venues throughout the region each summer. In 1936, the picnic was held at Swift's Beach in neighboring Wareham, where the group was captured in an informal photograph. One later chronicler wrote that although "not too heavily attended" that year, "we had a nice time." *Courtesy of Middleborough Historical Association.*

case for slips, dating stamps, record books, and instructed volunteers in their use." The branch was staffed by volunteers who included, over the years, Miss Rose Short, Eleanor Tompkins, Mrs. Frank Scienzo, Helen (Graham) Keller, Ruth (Freeman) Higgins, Corinne Cahoon, Mrs. Charles Trulson, Helen Thomas, Mrs. Arthur Harvey and Mrs. Chester Thomas. Serving as librarians were Mrs. George L. Finch, Mrs. Bessie Sweeney and Mrs. Perley Warren. Mrs. Sweeney, a daughter of Edward E. Sisson, served between 1944 and 1950 and was remembered by Jennie Gammons for bringing "to the library, by her free service, the warmth of generosity, a joy, which patrons feel, when they meet to exchange books." The branch library was noted for its home-like atmosphere, and it was "not unusual to see Mrs. Warren behind the desk with a child in her lap, after the mother was called out."

SCHOOL DAYS BETWEEN THE WARS

While the South Middleborough branch library helped cater to the educational needs of the community's adults, the South Middleborough School actively continued to fulfill that role for the area's children throughout the interwar period, despite the ever-present issue of overcrowding.

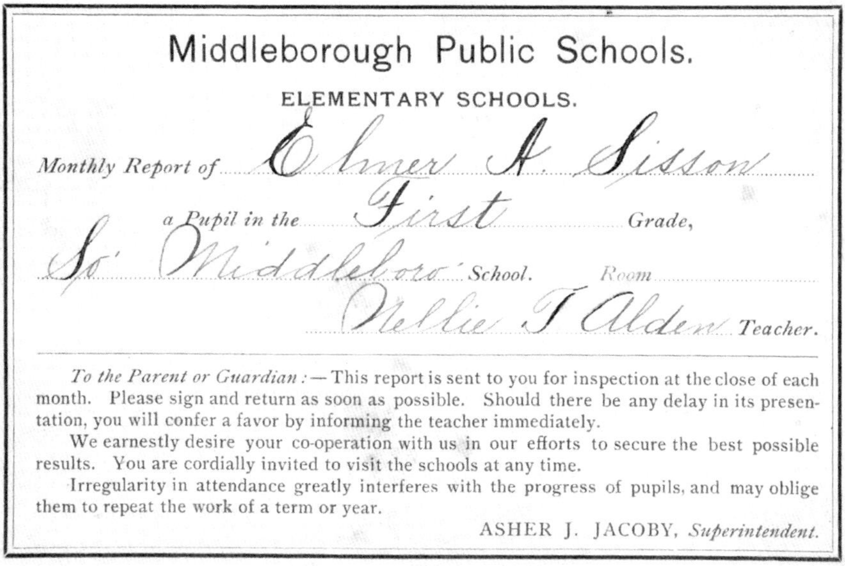

Middleborough Public Schools.

ELEMENTARY SCHOOLS.

Monthly Report of Elmer A. Sisson

a Pupil in the First *Grade,*

So' Middleboro' *School.* *Room*

Nellie T Alden *Teacher.*

To the Parent or Guardian:—This report is sent to you for inspection at the close of each month. Please sign and return as soon as possible. Should there be any delay in its presentation, you will confer a favor by informing the teacher immediately.

We earnestly desire your co-operation with us in our efforts to secure the best possible results. You are cordially invited to visit the schools at any time.

Irregularity in attendance greatly interferes with the progress of pupils, and may oblige them to repeat the work of a term or year.

ASHER J. JACOBY, *Superintendent.*

Despite the limitations of a one-room schoolhouse, students in South Middleborough received a comprehensive education, as indicated by the course work listed on Elmer A. Sisson's first grade report card from 1895. Reading, writing, spelling, language and composition, grammar, arithmetic, geography, elementary science, history, vocal music and drawing were all part of the local curriculum.

In 1921, Henry B. Burkland was engaged as the teacher for South Middleborough, and under his tutelage, the school flourished. Burkland would devote his life to the education of Middleborough's children, later serving as the town's middle school principal. His influence at South Middleborough was apparent in the scholars he helped prepare: "The 57 pupils in the 9 grades at South Middleboro proved to be exceptional pupils for the group to include two future teachers, two future selectmen, a dean, a gold-star soldier, etc."

When built in 1882, the South Middleborough schoolhouse had been the object of much admiration and pride as a thoroughly modern schoolhouse constructed in keeping with the tenets and principles of modern hygiene and education. This remained the case even decades later. Arad R. Dunham, who visited the school the day before Memorial Day 1917, indicated why: "The schoolyard was clean and neat, the house in perfect order and very well decorated for a season when flowers are so scarce." Nonetheless, by the time of the Second World War, the South Middleborough School had become archaic. The building remained heated by wood through the 1940s, and not until 1948 was a proper heating system installed. The lack of running water, too, branded the school as outmoded. For years, water had to be brought in pails from neighboring houses to the building, until the completion of a well. When the well experienced problems during the winter of 1935, the school had to resort to the former practice of trudging water from neighboring homes. In January 1942, a telephone was finally installed. Many of the improvements to the school were financed directly by the students, who were responsible for various fundraising activities. In 1920, the students were selling candy in order to finance playground improvements. The school was noted, in particular, for its annual pageants, usually held in later years at the neighboring fire station, during which each grade performed a separate feature.

Beyond the school playground, the vast woods and fields of South Middleborough provided ample opportunity for local children to play. In 1916, Herbert L. Wilber wrote of his younger brother Ralph's activities:

When this photograph of the South Middleborough School was taken in 1935, the building had become outmoded. Jennie Gammons described it as "weather-beaten drab with faded green trimmings and a dark roof." In 1948, a proper heating system replaced the wood stove, which "provides scorching heat in the front, but leaves cold nooks elsewhere." The community enlarged and modernized the building in the early 1950s. *Courtesy of Middleborough Historical Association.*

> *Ralph is making a great preparation for a party in the woods. He has made himself the captain of a new organization—the Rattlesnake Boy Scout patrol—They rattle tin cans with stones in them for a distinguishing mark. Ralph swiped my well-rope and then had the face to ask me to make a swing for him with it. I did.*

For older children, there was swimming and boating in the summer on Tispaquin Pond near Rock. Halloween was a particularly notable time of the year, when local children went about "with masks and lanterns" and were entertained by the Grange, though in 1919 Herbert L. Wilber noted the lack of "deviltry."

Closure of the South Middleborough Post Office and Railroad

Despite the expansion of South Middleborough's economy and the homely depiction of life in South Middleborough between the wars, circumstances were not good for all members of the community, and indications of an economic depression were evident in South Middleborough even prior to October 1929. "The low ebb in business compels residents to seek employment out of town," among them James and Frank Graham, Fred Buckman, Lewis Bradshaw and Edward Van Dusen. Some, simply unable to weather the mounting economic crisis of the 1930s, moved elsewhere, and few relief programs were provided to South Middleborough for those who remained. Though a new sidewalk was constructed in the autumn of 1939 as a WPA project, it became a metaphor for the temporariness of this relief effort. The sidewalk washed out the following fall and had to be rebuilt in the spring of 1941.

A potent economic sign of the times was the 1935 closing of the South Middleborough Post Office. Since 1892, when the Clark Store was removed to a new location, Ephraim H. Gammons had served as postmaster, with his wife as assistant. Upon her husband's death in 1926, Mrs. Gammons succeeded him as postmaster (1926), followed by her daughter, Jennie Gammons (1926–35). During this time, the Gammons House on Wareham Street served as the South Middleborough Post Office, located in the ell of the house where "a small room was fitted up with an outside entrance."

In 1892, the South Middleborough Post Office was moved from Clark's Corner to the Ephraim H. Gammons House on Wareham Street, near the South Middleborough Cemetery. Gammons served as postmaster from 1892 until his death in 1926; he was succeeded by his wife, Emma (1926), and daughter, Jennie M. (Gammons) Phillips (1926–35). In 1935, fourth-class post offices, including South Middleborough, were discontinued and replaced by the Rural Free Delivery system.

Though the post office operated day and night six days a week, frankly, not all residents were pleased with its relocation. "The arrangement did not suit everybody, for people had been in the habit of getting their mail at the store, where they went for groceries."

For years, the South Middleborough mail was carried by James Messroll, a character described by Jennie Gammons:

> *For years he trudged along, carpet bag in hand, to pick up mail at the store and from there to the post office to gather up the pouches for the train. He walked with a swaying motion of the sea. His face was tanned from exposure and one eye was sightless from an accident. Talking was his strong suit, wherever there was a listener, a stranger or otherwise...There came time in his 80s, when he was more meditative. He used a wheelbarrow, when mail pouches became heavy and he was obliged to rest on the handle-bars, for he was short of breath. He would say in a careless tone, "Seems to me, I'm goin' to another planet." That event happened at the age of 84, but he lives, like a character in fiction.*

Messroll was succeeded by E. Howard Shaw, who transported the mail by automobile but had problems of his own, according to Jennie Gammons. "Pouches were thrown from a fast moving train and the landing place varied. On a dark night a search of the track was often necessary or his parked car may have been a target. The train caught mail bags from a crane and timing was important for placing them in position before that metal arm was outstretched. The delay of seconds meant danger." Shaw served until the post office was abolished in 1935, at which time South Middleborough was placed on Rural Free Delivery Route 2.

The Depression would also bring an even more significant change to South Middleborough with the demise of rail service. In 1933, the station's Railway Express Agency office was closed, following which express business was conducted from Rock. Finally, in 1938, the New Haven announced the discontinuation of service on its Cape Division and the closing of all stations along that line, including South Middleborough. "Every mile of the Old Colony Railroad is today paralleled by a modern, heavy-duty highway. As

During the time that it was located in the Gammons House, the South Middleborough Post Office was entered through this door at the side of the house, marked by a small, unpretentious sign. South Middleborough residents were initially resistant to the removal of the post office from Clark's Corner, so accustomed had they been to picking up their mail at the South Middleborough store. *Courtesy of Middleborough Historical Association.*

Like other local railroads, the Cape Cod branch subsisted primarily on freight receipts with little passenger traffic originating in South Middleborough. As a consequence of the decline of the lumber industry following 1910 and the rise of alternative means of freighting, the South Middleborough station closed in the late 1930s. The passenger depot, seen here at that time, was later relocated to Benson Street and converted into a residential dwelling.

a result, the railroad has had taken from it practically all the local traffic which it was primarily built to handle." Also cited was increased competition from new bus lines. The announcement brought immediate protests from the community at South Middleborough, but backed by a ruling of the Massachusetts Supreme Court, the railroad remained unmoved. The South Middleborough station never reopened.

The closure of the South Middleborough station proved to be an economic blow for the community, as for years many local residents had been employed by the railroad. Noteworthy was F.L. Wallen, who served as the station agent at South Middleborough from 1876 to 1922. James Boucher and Clifford Westgate of Rock later served in that capacity. Section bosses responsible for the upkeep and maintenance of the line along a certain designated portion of the road, as well as the extinguishing of fires in their sections, included William O. LeBaron, John Smith, Harry LeBaron and Joseph Boutin, who were assisted by section workers, including Ernest Bearse, Henry Wilcox and George Pische. In addition to the loss of these jobs, the remaining depot facilities at South Middleborough were gradually dismantled. By the end of July 1940, little remained to indicate that a station had ever stood there: "Seems as though the railroad service was blotted out forever," commented the local South Middleborough correspondent of the *Middleboro Gazette*.

Conservatism and the Precinct Three Improvement Association

Helping South Middleborough weather the loss of institutions such as the post office and railroad station that had once contributed to the identity of the village was its strong sense of community and its deeply held values. During the post–World War I era, a strong sense of political and social conservatism continued to pervade the South Middleborough community. Politically, the community at South Middleborough remained avowedly Republican, voting overwhelmingly in favor of political candidates from that party, in greater proportion even than the town as a whole. Harold A. Williams deftly defined the community's political conservatism in 1946 by joking that "the only Democrat down here is a registered Republican."

The community's conservative values, its continuing dissatisfaction with the course of local spending, the poor economic climate of the time and the loss of particular institutions such as its post office and railroad station culminated in the formation of the Precinct Three Improvement Association, which was founded on the same sensibility dominant in South Middleborough following the Civil War—a distinct perception of being short-changed by town government. Upon the association's organization on November 21, 1938, the *Middleboro Gazette* noted, "Those in the southern portion of the town pay a large assessment of taxes, and feel that they are entitled to receive such benefits as may be commensurate with taxes paid into the town treasury from this section." The role of the Improvement Association was to identify these benefits and to lobby actively for them. Ultimately, the association would request the continuation of train service, an extension of municipal water, improved sidewalks, the establishment of a branch library, the presence of a fire warden, maintenance of its roadways, installation of traffic lights and prohibition of the fluoridation of the municipal water supply. Though not successful in all of these efforts, the Improvement Association was a vital link in the historic continuity of South Middleborough, joining as it did the anti-tax separatist sentiments and actions of the late nineteenth century with

Throughout the interwar period, the South Middleborough Methodist Church remained a unifying influence that continued to provide the community with an identity. Easter 1934 was celebrated in the church by eighty-three people, though not all are captured in this view. Pastor S.J.A. Rook stands at the podium flanked by the senior choir to the left and the junior choir to the right. *Courtesy of Middleborough Historical Association.*

the present-day South Middleboro Protective Association. The activities of the Improvement Association and its progress, however, were interrupted by American involvement in the Second World War following the Japanese attack on Pearl Harbor on December 7, 1941.

WORLD WAR II AND THE "BOMBING" OF SOUTH MIDDLEBOROUGH

Prior to the outbreak of war in December 1941, South Middleborough had been exposed to wartime preparedness procedures. In June, soldiers from Camp Edwards on Cape Cod had engaged in maneuvers in the vicinity, and a number of South Middleborough residents had enlisted in the armed forces, including Russell Tripp and Everett W. Collins. The community itself began preparations by naming Everett Buckman as air raid warden for South Middleborough, with Harold Williams as his assistant, in the late summer of 1941. The community was also included in the distribution of so-called bomb sand on March 14, 1942. Middleborough Highway

Ralph Gordon Wilber, the son of Herbert L. and Edith Wilber, was one of many South Middleborough men and women to serve during World War II. Wilber is pictured beneath the red astrakhan apple tree in the rear of the Wilber home on Wareham Street in May 1944. *Courtesy of Middleborough Historical Association.*

Department trucks distributed sand to congested areas where homes were clustered closely together. Sand was to be kept readily available in metal buckets "for use in extinguishing and disposing of incendiary bombs." It is not clear how readily South Middleborough residents participated. The *Gazette* reported that only 30 percent of householders outside the center had put out pails to be filled, while the percentage for the center (50 percent) was not much better.

Lackluster participation in the sand distribution program fueled concerns about preparedness in the event of an air raid, particularly since the town had held only one blackout drill in May 1941 prior to the start of the war. Accordingly, both air raid defense tests and test blackouts started to be scheduled with regularity. Initially, the bell of the South Middleborough church was to be used to supplement the town's two existing fire alarm sirens located in Middleborough center to signal an air raid, though this was superseded in June 1942, when an electric air raid whistle was installed in Sisson's Garage, operated by the same compressed air system that Sisson used to inflate tires.

Though necessary precautions, air raid defense drills played havoc with Cape traffic on Route 28. On Sunday, March 29, 1942, over 225 northbound cars were halted at the Middleborough line in Rochester while "some 56 additional that had passed the town line before the start of the blackout were stopped in lower South Middleboro." Despite the inconvenience, "the drivers cooperated without protest." Additional town blackouts were conducted on April 7, 1942; in August 1942; and on June 23–24, 1943, along with two statewide blackouts held on December 15, 1942, and February 28, 1943.

On Monday, May 11, 1943, the evening before registration for gasoline rationing was to commence, Middleborough's defense organizations participated in a rehearsal mobilization, though without a blackout, in which South Middleborough was actively engaged. A second surprise test was conducted late Sunday afternoon, June 21, during which an imaginary enemy bomber was shot down by an interceptor plane at 5:10 p.m., crashing some five hundred yards north of the South Middleborough railroad station, east of the tracks to Cape Cod. Three men were "seen" parachuting from the plane and "have landed near Wareham street nearly opposite the burning plane." The State Guard was dispatched to capture the men. During this raid, the recently installed electric air raid siren at Sisson's gas station was employed for the first time.

More disconcerting was a bomb scare in November 1944, when a terrible blast shook windows at Sisson's Garage and Diner, Lucy Braley's and homes in the neighborhood, prompting residents to fear a "robot bomb." Following an investigation by Chief of Police Alden C. Sisson, local fears were allayed. The blast, in fact, was associated with the construction of a cranberry bog west of the railroad tracks.

Rationing and Salvage Drives

Rationing was a wartime development that touched everyone, including the residents of South Middleborough, when a variety of goods came under strict government regulation. Residents were required to register for a war ration book during the first week of May 1942, and in order to facilitate this process, local schools, including the South Middleborough School, were closed on Monday, May 4. The following day, sugar rationing went into effect, with retailers such as Thomas Brothers' and industrial users like Lucy Braley's having registered in late April. All sugar sales were frozen for two weeks starting on April 27, after which each resident was permitted half a pound of sugar per week. On June 9, 1942, a deputy rationing board responsible for distributing supplementary sugar rations was named for South Middleborough and Rock consisting of Richmond Matthews (chairman), Mrs. Alice Pope, Bertha Beers and Sylvester Greene. A week later, the deputy board's overview was restricted to South Middleborough when a separate board was named for Rock.

Gasoline rationing began on May 16, with registration starting on May 12. Once again, the South Middleborough School was closed on the first day of registration. Other rationed items included new automobile tires (February 1942), typewriters (March 1942), bicycles (May 1942), rubber footwear (September 1942), fuel oil (October 1942), coffee (November 1942), canned goods (February 1943), shoes (February 1943), meat (March 1943), fat (March 1943), processed fish (March 1943) and cheese (March 1943). Retailers like Thomas Brothers' were required to file price lists for certain commodities with the local War Price and Rationing Board by July 1. Fuel conservation saw the closing of schools statewide for two weeks until March 18, 1943, in an effort to conserve fuel.

As a rural community, South Middleborough, like other areas outside Middleborough center, had unique problems, and in April 1942, a nine-member Rural War Action Committee was established in Middleborough to address rural concerns, with Agnes Buckman and William MacDougall representing South Middleborough. Food remained a preoccupation of homefront war preparedness efforts, and in early 1942, Agnes Buckman and Mrs. Leslie M. Woodward were named by the Extension Service to provide residents with information on nutrition, home gardens and food preservation. The South Middleborough Grange contributed with

THE METHODIST YOUTH
FELLOWSHIP
of the South Middleboro Church
presents
MANPOWER
SHORTAGE
A comedy in Three Acts
Written by
Dorothy and Philip Wilber
South Middleboro Grange Hall
April 26, 1944
8:00 P.M.

Church-sponsored entertainments remained an important part of the South Middleborough community throughout the war era, as evidenced by the Methodist Youth Fellowship's 1944 production of *Manpower Shortage*, written by Dorothy and Philip Wilber and performed at the South Middleborough Grange Hall. The three-act play was described as "very good, and at times killingly funny," and the Grange Hall was "well filled" for the production. *Courtesy of Middleborough Historical Association.*

lectures on similar topics in 1942, as well as Victory Home Food Supply and Victory Food Production contests in the spring of 1943. Canning demonstrations were held in the vestry of the Methodist church and were reportedly "well attended."

Salvage and scrap drives remained an important means of collecting well-needed war-related materials while boosting local homefront morale. Residents were solicited to contribute metal, rags, wastepaper, rubber and automobile batteries. Beginning in September 1943, tin cans were collected, and residents were encouraged to deposit them at the junction of Wareham and Pine Streets, as well as opposite Thomas Brothers' store.

War preparedness also saw the community provided with courses in first aid, lessons being conducted by A. Whitman Higgins, assisted by Agnes Buckman and Gladys Houlihan, and held at the Scout Cabin. While residents who took the course fortunately never needed to use their training in hostile situations, it did prove useful. When Mrs. Lewis Short's younger son fell while climbing and broke a collarbone in July 1942, Mrs. Short "found the knowledge she had learned, came in handy, until she could get a doctor."

Local women participated in Red Cross work, including mending for St. Luke's Hospital in Middleborough and the preparation of surgical dressings made in the church vestry throughout 1943. Additionally, a number of women, including Agnes Buckman, Alice Pope, Florence Wilbur and Mabel Thomas, went to Middleborough each week to prepare dressings. The Precinct Three Improvement Association, whose lobbying activities had gone into abeyance for the duration of the war, devoted its efforts toward war preparedness as well. In May 1942, the association invited Horace Atkins to "show pictures on Defense."

Concentration on the war effort was total, and some began to have concerns regarding the potentially adverse impact that this focus might have on younger members of the community. Reverend Lamb of the South Middleborough church cautioned that focus on the war effort should not be allowed to overtake focus on the family. Speaking before the Bates School PTA in September 1943, Reverend Lamb discussed what he considered "the great mistake in not keeping the intimacy of the home the center of interest for children growing up in this war-torn age" and stated that parents should teach "discipline, the meaning of work, good manners and courtesy, the worth of money, good health, and self reliance" to children. "He closed with the thought that juvenile delinquency was caused by adult delinquency, a challenge to parents today whose only concern seems to be the war effort."

South Middleborough's Servicemen and Women

As ever, South Middleborough in the early 1940s remained a closely knit community, and the common cause of war only strengthened that bond, with residents keenly concerned for the welfare of their men and women in the armed services. To help maintain that connection, a book was placed in the vestibule of the Methodist church recording the names and addresses of local residents in service to whom members of the community were urged to write. At Christmas 1943, Reverend Lamb suggested the community write to its servicemen and women, and accordingly their addresses were published in the weekly church calendar, beginning with that of Private Leslie Thomas. In February 1944, a new American flag was dedicated and hung in the church auditorium, and in July 1944, plans called for placing photographs of those South Middleborough residents in service in the

In December 1944, a vesper service was held in the South Middleborough church as a tribute to the community's youths then serving in the armed forces. The committee in charge of the candlelight included (from left to right) Mrs. Leslie M. Woodward, Miss Annie H. Wilbur, Reverend Glen W. Lamb, A. Whitman Higgins and Mrs. Fred Buckman. *Courtesy of Sharon Higgins Cope-Carriere.*

church. The church sent Christmas boxes to local servicemen and women in 1943 and was collecting funds to repeat the effort in 1944 with hopes "to be able to send as nice boxes as last year."

Those South Middleborough residents serving in the armed forces during the war included: Alfred P. Alberti, Kenneth Beaton, Robert L. Burnham, Everett W. Collins, Robert H. Donovan, Toivo Erickson, Dwight M. Fowler, Doris E. Freeman, James C. Graham, Whitman W. Higgins, Perley A. Hollis, Robert F. Johnson, Nilo Liukko, Melville T. Matthews, Harold C. Minkle, Robert M. Pope, Herman E. Russell, Marjorie A. Shaw, LeRoy Sweeney, Leslie W. Thomas, Winthrop S. Thomas, Russell W. Tripp, Maurice E. Warren, Perley S. Warren, Donald T. Welch, Ralph G. Wilber, Ralph W. Wilbur and Harold H. Williams.

South Middleborough's sole World War II casualty was Sergeant Russell W. Tripp, son of Ralph W. Tripp of Benson Street. Tripp served in the Tenth Armored Division of Patton's Third Army in Germany and was killed on March 1, 1945, eight days prior to his twenty-seventh birthday. Tripp had volunteered on May 26, 1941.

Agitation for Fire Protection

Prior to the war, South Middleborough had begun to agitate for better municipal services in the form of municipal water and improved fire protection. Demand for water had always been an issue in South Middleborough, with periodic droughts causing wells to dry and fields to parch, most notably in 1912, 1919, 1922, 1923 and 1941. Consequently, the extension of a municipal waterline to South Middleborough was deemed a priority. Coupled with this was an insistence on improved fire protection for the community. Though agitation for public water was abandoned with the outbreak of war (it would finally be secured at mid-century), South Middleborough continued to call for better fire protection following 1941, largely through the agency of the Precinct Three Improvement Association, which requested that a deputy fire warden be appointed for the precinct and that a piece of forest fire–fighting equipment be stationed there as well. Though Middleborough Board of Selectmen chairman James F. Shurtleff flatly stated that there was no money available with which to purchase such a piece of apparatus, South Middleborough would acquire its much sought-after fire engine somewhat unexpectedly in 1943 as the result of a dispute between the Middleborough Fire Department and the State Department of Conservation, which at that time was housing a pumper at the Central Fire Station in Middleborough, "equipped with two pumps, hose and other forest fighting equipment, and…an armored front for breaking through undergrowth."

Contrary to its agreement with the Conservation Department, the town failed to provide a driver for the engine, concerned that the driver, needed in Middleborough, might be called for duty outside the town. District Fire Warden Farnham, already on record as gravely concerned with the fire protection in the southern section of town, had the engine removed to South Middleborough, where it was placed in charge of Harold A. Williams, deputy fire warden, and housed in Sisson's Garage. The engine saw frequent duty battling wood fires primarily east and southeast of South Middleborough until May 5, 1944, when it was destroyed in a dramatic fire in the Myles Standish State Forest at Plymouth, from which Williams and crew member Dura Higgins barely escaped.

With the loss of the state pumper, South Middleborough was once again without a piece of firefighting apparatus. Consequently, the community took

A dispute between the Massachusetts Department of Conservation and the Middleborough Fire Department resulted in the removal of the state's brush-breaker to South Middleborough. The engine was South Middleborough's first piece of fire apparatus and was housed in the Sisson barn on Locust Street. Here, deputy fire warden Harold A. Williams poses with the engine about 1944 outside the Sisson House. *Courtesy of Middleborough Historical Association.*

it upon itself to build its own engine from scratch. Elmer A. Sisson donated a dump truck chassis, a Ford V-8 engine and funds; Harold F. Peck of the Square Deal Garage in Wareham provided two tanks with a combined capacity of 595 gallons; and a truck body was received from Rochester. The pumper was assembled during June 1944 by Sisson, Harold A. Williams, James E. Graham, William Greely, Samuel Brown and Dura Higgins.

At the time of the pumper's construction, the men sought $1,000 for a pump and one thousand feet of hose with which to outfit the engine, prompting the local newspaper to patronizingly chide:

> *If the South Middleboro group had been a little more forethoughtful they might have had the matter before the voters at the special town meeting held Monday night. All they needed to do was present a petition signed by 10 or more voters, to the selectmen before the warrant was made up.*

What the *Gazette* so glaringly failed to recognize was that South Middleborough was the only area of town where the community felt compelled to provide its own fire protection from its own financial resources, something residents believed their taxes should be providing. As Harold A. Williams said simply, "At least we are trying to help ourselves."

Largely through the lobbying efforts of South Middleborough's Precinct Three Improvement Association, fire protection for outlying districts of

Middleborough, not just South Middleborough, increasingly became a subject on the local political agenda. Selectmen candidates Alfred M. Butler, in 1945, and Otto P. Becker Jr., in 1948, both advocated improved fire protection for the outlying areas of Middleborough with fire apparatus to be stationed there. Unfortunately for advocates of improved fire protection, neither was elected.

The *Gazette* simply scoffed at such propositions, obtusely arguing that the existing Central Fire Station at Middleborough was better able to protect outlying districts than could outlying stations. South Middleborough residents, however, did not necessarily share the *Gazette*'s buoyant optimism. While certainly confident in the abilities of the Middleborough Fire Department, South Middleborough residents were concerned about their distance from Middleborough center and the delays that might be encountered, a natural trepidation born of actual experience. On August 15, 1927, the Capeway Tourist Camp located on Wareham Street, midway between Houdlett's Corner and the Rochester line, was leveled largely due to the response time required from Middleborough center. Though a fire the following January 1928 at the White Arbor Tea Room was put out and the building saved, it was reported to have been only "a few minutes" from destruction when the fire department propitiously arrived from Middleborough center. Valuable time was lost, once more, in responding to a call from Middleborough center in January 1930 when the fire department hastily appeared at a house across from Thomas's store in Rock but was perplexed to find no fire. The fire was, in fact, in the James M. Clark House across the road from Thomas Brothers' store *in South Middleborough*. While the department eventually arrived on the scene and quenched the minor fire, it proved a valuable example to South Middleborough residents of the need for more local fire protection.

South Middleboro Protective Association and Fire Station

Ultimately, years of frustrated ambition would culminate in the establishment of the South Middleboro Protective Association, which fostered the formation of an independent fire company in South Middleborough and the construction of its own station between 1955 and 1957, all indications of just how truly self-reliant the community had learned to become.

Construction of the station commenced in 1955, and would take some two years to complete since it was largely a volunteer effort. Elmer Sisson later recalled Reverend Lester Moore, "clad in overalls, [as] the first volunteer on the scene. He chopped down trees until 9 a. m., and then shed his overalls for the vestments of the clergy and preached a sermon in the little white church across the road."

The construction of the station proceeded, according to the *Middleboro Gazette*, "with typical South Middleboro persistence." Following the pouring of thirty-one yards of concrete, the walls were framed and boarded with rough sawn boards. "Everyone laughed at those boards," Elmer Sisson would later recall. Nonetheless, they were soon covered with tarpaper, and fieldstones were piled against the walls, one Sunday witnessing seventeen loads of stones going into the walls of the building.

South Middleborough residents would later construct their own engine from scrap parts and donated materials and manned a volunteer firefighting force staffed by local residents, including "Bud" Matthews and Bill Greeley, who here demonstrate the equipment to a young Dura Higgins. The group is captured outside the Sisson House on Locust Street, the barn of which served as South Middleborough's first fire station. *Courtesy of Middleborough Historical Association.*

By 1956, the station was operating with one call captain and twelve call men. In October 1957, two semi-trailer trucks were donated to South Middleborough by James A. Collins of the Collins Transportation Company of Taunton. In 1972, in an action harkening back to earlier days, the South Middleborough firefighters built their own brush-breaker. The new engine was completed from the body of a retired brush-breaker; the secondhand engine, cab and chassis of an old 1964 Ford fish truck; steel sections from an earlier forest fire truck; and "heavy steel angle irons," ironically once part of the fire tower at Sandwich and acquired from a secondhand junk dealer. Their previous brush-breaker, a 1946 Ford, had originally been a secondhand oil truck that had been purchased for $100.

Postwar Residential and Commercial Growth

With the renewed availability of materials for residential home construction following 1945, several new houses were constructed in South Middleborough in the period immediately following the war, signaling the continuing optimism in the community as a desirable residential neighborhood. Houses for Raymond C. Perry, Kenneth Wilbur, Lawrence A. Cannon, Melville T. Matthews and William L. Greely were all raised during this period. As all of these men had connections with South Middleborough, it still could be argued that South Middleborough remained a community of closely knit families.

Besides residential construction, the immediate postwar era also saw new commercial construction in the form of a modern store building for Thomas Brothers' store. Following the February 1929 death of Lyman P. Thomas, Thomas Brothers' had been reorganized in May 1929, with the two remaining partners—Alfred and Alvin E. Thomas—taking into partnership clerks Elliott G. Beaton of West Wareham and Richmond C. Matthews. In 1938, Alvin Thomas sold his share of the business to Gilbert C. Phinney. Phinney and Beaton retired, and on April 1, 1944, Harlan L. Matthews became a partner with his brother, Richmond. In 1947, the two Matthews brothers decided that a new facility was needed to replace the large store building that had served for the past half century. Accordingly, land on Wareham Street for a new Thomas Brothers' store was purchased on December 1, 1947, from Mrs. Florence Williams, and a modern store

Continual modernization allowed the Thomas Brothers' store at Clark's Corner to cater successfully to South Middleborough shoppers such as Edith and Dorothy Wilber, who are here being assisted on February 1, 1935, by Elliott Beaton, Stuart Rose and Alfred Thomas. Though Thomas Brothers' sold the store shortly after this photograph was taken, the name was retained. Thirteen years later, the firm relocated to Wareham Street. *Courtesy of Middleborough Historical Association.*

opened for business on May 20, 1948. The building "was well stocked with everything in the grocery line, neatly packaged for handling or self-service. Frozen goods were supplied for customers who had acquired a taste for such delicacies." The business was discontinued in March 1959 by Matthews's son Melville, prompting the *Gazette* to remark, "This is the first time for many years that South Middleborough has been without a grocery store." Briefly during 1949, the former Thomas Brothers' store at Clark's Corner became the home of a museum devoted to Tom Thumb, the diminutive performer made famous by P.T. Barnum. Operated by Benjamin and Edna Bump, the small museum was relocated after a season to Edaville Railroad in Carver.

Adjoining the new Thomas Brothers' store was another family-owned and operated business, Williams Trading Post, which was established in 1949 by Harold A. Williams. In April 1999, Martha (Williams) Dupuis recalled the start of the business by her grandfather fifty years earlier:

> *In the spring of 1949 Harold Astor Williams was recovering from an illness and surgery. Harold, or "Grandpa," as our generation knew him,*

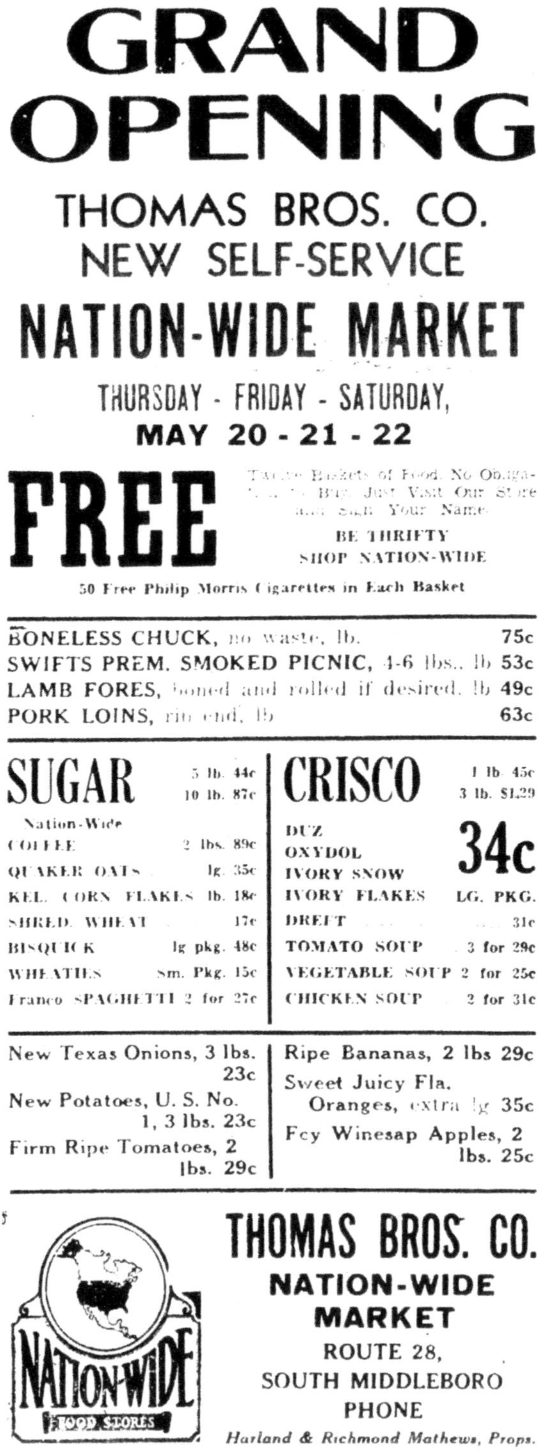

Encouraged by the modern development of the retail grocery trade, Thomas Brothers' owners Harland L. and Richmond C. Matthews acquired a lot of land fronting Wareham Street between Lucy Braley's Candy Kitchen and Williams Trading Post for construction of a new store that was opened in May 1948, at which time the wood-frame store at Clark's Corner was abandoned.

was ready to work on a part-time basis as he entered the retirement years of his life. With his wife, Florence by his side (not sure who was the "real boss"), a few boxes of pansies were set out on display on wooden crates and old wash stands. This was the beginning.

The business offered fresh produce grown by the Williams family and profited by its location on the route to Cape Cod. Williams's children, Harold Hunt ("Buzzie") Williams and Ellen (Williams) Taylor, assisted with the business. "Over the years roofs were added, leaving space for the trees to grow up through the roofline, and additional buildings erected. The 'annex'

Established in 1949 by Harold A. and Florence (Hunt) Williams to market some of the family's home-grown flowers and produce, Williams Trading Post evolved into South Middleborough's most successful and longest-lived business and is now operated successfully by the couple's granddaughter, Martha (Williams) Dupuis. The post is well known for its colorful and attractive floral displays each spring and fall and remains a landmark on Route 28.

housed gift items, fabrics, and houseplants for many years. Textiles had been [Harold Williams's] original career path."

Yet another small retail operation was established in 1951 by Basil K. Neftel on Wareham Street immediately north of the former Hell's Blazes Tavern. Originally, the store retailed farm equipment, paints and hardware, but in 1952, the Neftels received a liquor license to operate the store as a package store known as the Town Line Package Store. The operation of the store was restricted to "the sale of packaged liquors, bait and tackle, marine supplies and boats, and a gift shop, excluding any items of food, excepting potato chips and like items usually incidental to the sale of packaged liquors." Still later, the Neftels operated the store as a gift shop known as the Christmas Shop.

Despite growing uncertainty regarding the economic future of South Middleborough, businesses continued to be established. In 1956–57, Peter A. and Muriel M. Cammarata constructed a restaurant on a vacant plot of land midway between the site of Benson's sawmill and the Stillman Benson House. The restaurant, like many of South Middleborough's businesses, operated seasonally, generally running between April and October. A second restaurant opened at this time was the White & Gold House, constructed about 1958 just north of Williams Trading Post and operated as a restaurant catering to Cape-bound motorists, owned by Germaine Doucette and James Gotham Jr. It was described in October 1959 as "a modern new building of white and gold without and white and gold within accented with touches of pink to set the mood." A relatively small building, the restaurant seated fifty customers at a time. The slogan of the restaurant was: "Good Food for Families and Friends."

During this period, the former Hell's Blazes Tavern was revitalized by Basil K. and Martha E. Neftel and catered to summer tourists on the way to and from the Cape. In September 1952, the Neftels sold the property to Fred L. and Mary B. Turnbull of West Hartford, Connecticut. The Turnbulls painted the weathered gray historic structure chocolate brown and installed red awnings, conducting the restaurant as Travellers' Fare. The tavern's owner after March 1957, John Paul Stack, "former New York hotel executive," proposed operating the tavern seasonally between early June and October 1 and creating a fifty-room addition "in the nature of motel facilities." The addition was never realized, although the restaurant remained popular.

Less substantial in size was the Cape Cod Do-Nut Shop, operated in the late 1940s by Henry L. and Martha L.E. Koepfer. Clearly, given its name, this was a business intended to cater to passing tourists. Constructed on a relatively secluded stretch of Wareham Street between Pine Street and the Rochester line, the shop could not hope to prosper solely from local traffic. Just a short distance south was located a small picnic ground situated in a bend in a discontinued portion of Wareham Street and maintained by the state. Here, in 1952, Manuel Centeio of Carver manufactured and sold ice cream.

Postwar developments in the provision of lodging took a drastic step forward when the first motel in Middleborough was built by Winifred Perry on the parcel to the north of Williams Trading Post. The operation was crude by modern standards (shower stalls were located directly in a corner of each room) but a vast improvement on the earlier overnight camps that had been the norm prior to the war. Nonetheless, the venture was short-lived as the expectations of travelers rapidly advanced throughout the decade that followed. More in keeping with the modern conception of the motel was the Alpine Motel and Snack Bar, built in 1954 by partners Stephen Apostolos

"Motor hotels," or motels, developed during World War II and were an advance on earlier motor camps and tourist cabins. Stephen and Mary Apostolos (with their daughter Jane) operated the first modern motel in South Middleborough as the Alpine Motel. As part of the operation, the family conducted a snack bar situated at the front of the motel facing Wareham Street. *Courtesy of Dan and Jane (Apostolos) Thompson.*

and Arthur Kamberis on Wareham Street just south of Houdlett's Corner. The Alpine was contemporary with the Peterson Motel, built by Lemuel Peterson that same year a few miles north on Wareham Street, and the two operations represented an increasingly professional take on the provision of overnight accommodations. The Alpine Motel—the name an allusion to the tract of white pines that surrounded it—was built specifically to cater to Cape traffic, and it was long operated by Apostolos and his wife, Mary.

The Continuing Sense of Community

Throughout the postwar period, South Middleborough's remaining institutions would continue to strengthen both the sense of community in South Middleborough as well as the perception of community as independent and highly self-reliant. To the South Middleborough School, church and Grange as unifying and identifying organizations could now be added the Precinct Three Improvement Association and the local fire squad.

Activities in South Middleborough continued to be community focused throughout the mid-twentieth century. In 1958, South Middleborough initiated a community fair, with various local organizations, including Engine 6, the Women's Auxiliary, the South Middleborough Grange and the South Middleboro Skating Club, participating. These fairs, held for a number of years on the grounds of the fire station, provided yet another example of the community spiritedness of South Middleborough. To this might also be added the South Middleboro Community Scholarship Fund, which was established to benefit residents of the Third Precinct.

Community athletic activities were revived at the parsonage with the creation of a baseball field there. "The young people have been busy mowing, raking and cutting down bushes at the ball field on the parsonage grounds, getting it in readiness for ball practice and games," noted the *Middleboro Gazette* in July 1959. This same field was utilized in August 1959 for a morning worship service. Local teams continued to utilize the field for a number of years.

Yet another noteworthy example of South Middleborough's community spirit was the development of the South Middleboro Skating Club in the 1950s. For generations, Hunt's Pond, a small pond situated between the Smith-LeBaron-Hunt House on Locust Street and Route 28 and ringed by

The daughter of Ephraim H. and Emma Gammons, Jennie Gammons (1874–1964) was the first South Middleborough woman to obtain a college education and was noted for her longevity as a local newspaper correspondent. Here she is seen in 1961, celebrating the 200th anniversary of organized religion in South Middleborough in the company of Reverend Manley Shaw (district supervisor), Bishop Mathews and Reverend Donald N. Broughton. *Courtesy of Middleborough Historical Association.*

trees, was the scene of innumerable skating-related diversions, including ice hockey. In 1929, a team of South Middleborough boys comprising Snowden Thomas, Maurice Goodell, Richard Van Dusen, Harvey MacNeill and Malcolm Foster defeated a team from Rock, 8–7. More formalized community skating was inaugurated by Harold A. Williams, who "set about adding improvements, electric lights, a record player, for youths liked to skate at night after the youngsters had gone to bed," recalled Jennie Gammons. In September 1962, a new clubhouse was constructed for the group, and in 1968–69, the club first sponsored a youth hockey team known as the Flyers as part of the Old Colony Boys Amateur Hockey League, organized for boys under age nineteen and attending school. Sadly, with the opening of indoor rinks in Brockton and Taunton in the 1970s, Hunt's Pond fell into disuse, and the skating club became defunct, one of a growing number of South Middleborough institutions that would cease following the mid-1960s.

6
SOUTH MIDDLEBOROUGH SINCE 1966

It was something terrible. It was as if a big black curtain lowered.
—Lucy (Braley) Sisson on the opening of Route 25

With the construction of yet another highway, Route 25, which was designed simply to facilitate the flow of traffic along the Cape route, ease congestion and reduce accidents along Route 28 but ultimately had the impact of bypassing South Middleborough, the community entered a period of economic decline as businesses established during the twentieth-century expansion began to succumb to economic pressures. Coupled with this was the closure of those institutions that had for so many years provided the community with an identity: the South Middleborough branch library and the South Middleborough School. The new identity that began to succeed its former one was not entirely welcome, as South Middleborough became the object of consideration for developments not particularly wanted elsewhere in Middleborough, a situation exacerbated by the general-use zoning adopted at this time. By 1990, with the South Middleborough School closed and most of its business departed, the community reached the threshold of a new era in its history and sought to define a new role for itself.

ROUTE 25 AND THE CRANBERRY HIGHWAY ASSOCIATION

The first indication that Route 28 through South Middleborough was to be superceded came in 1952 when a new highway between the Fall River–Boston Expressway (Route 24) to the Middleborough rotary was discussed as the first portion of a divided high-speed highway route from Boston to Cape Cod. Eventually designated as Route 25 in April 1961, this new expressway was proposed to bypass South Middleborough, a possibility that prompted local residents as early as September 1952 to call for the upgrading rather than the replacement of Route 28. For nearly fifteen years, South Middleborough business owners would fight against the opening of the new highway.

Though many residents approved of the proposal from the point of view of improved safety, as the new road would do away with the "old Route 28's numerous, fatality-strewn curves [and] the old, 'Russian Roulette' layout;

By 1951, when this photograph was taken looking toward the intersection of Locust and Wareham Streets after a heavy winter storm, Route 28 had become a heavily trafficked roadway and the scene of numerous accidents. In the background (from left to right) are the Sisson House, Sisson Filling Station and Garage, Lucy Braley's Candy Kitchen and the Thomas Brothers' store. *Courtesy of Sharon Higgins Cope-Carriere.*

a seemingly haphazard pattern of shifting lanes and opposing traffic," the proposed Route 28 bypass was strongly opposed by local businesses, which argued that it would "strangle" business. "Most motorists would have no reason to turn onto the old route 28 with the modern superhighway spanning the same points," it was argued in June 1955. In response to these fears, the Cranberry Highway Association (with a number of South Middleborough businesses among its members) was formed in 1959 to staunch the flow of traffic from the older route between the Middleborough rotary and Orleans on Cape Cod. In the spring of 1959, the association was instrumental in having Route 28 between the Middleborough rotary and its termination at Orleans on Cape Cod officially designated by the commonwealth as the Cranberry Highway. While the association sponsored a number of high-profile events and promoted local businesses, the hype surrounding these developments would not prove successful when contrasted with the convenience Route 25 offered modern motorists, who were more eager to reach their destination than to enjoy their travel to it.

Lucy Braley Tackles Massachusetts Blue Laws

A second development at this time that further constrained South Middleborough business was the revived enforcement of Massachusetts's so-called blue laws, one of which prohibited all but necessary businesses from opening on Sundays. Particularly sharp in her critique of the blue laws in South Middleborough was Lucy Braley Sisson, who (also clearly angered by the proposed opening of Route 25) questioned, "Isn't it enough that people who have built up businesses on certain highways are cut off peremptorily by the new super highways? Must we have insult added to injury by being told, in effect, 'Look, you fool; you don't know what necessary means. We'll tell you'?"

Mrs. Sisson refused to shutter her business on Sundays and, returning home from a weekend away, discovered that she had been visited in her absence by a member of the state police. Sisson immediately sent a lengthy letter to the *Middleboro Gazette* in which she took particular issue with the antiquated law that stated, "Whoever on the Lord's Day keeps open his shop, warehouse, or workhouse or does any manner of labor, business, or work, except works of necessity and charity, shall be punished by a fine of fifty dollars."

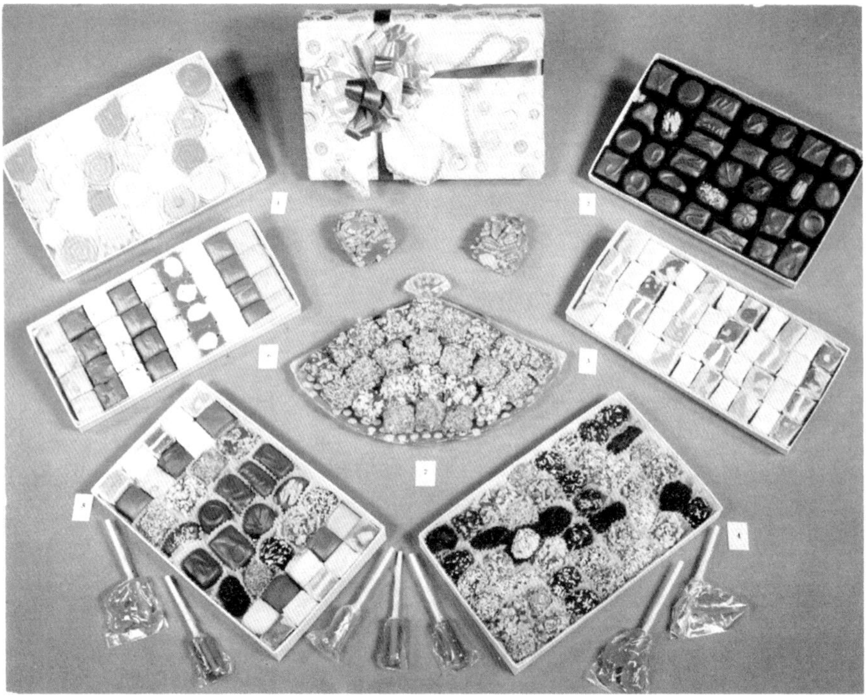

This photograph was used by Lucy Braley's Candy Kitchen to promote the variety of candy and sweets it produced, including assorted chocolates, cream mints, cream rolls, caramels, nougats, fudge and "barley pops." The operation employed a number of advertising tag lines over the years, including the "Home of Home Made Candies" and "The Gift of Good Taste," revealing an increasingly modern business approach for this one-time roadside stand.

> *I say every day is the Lord's Day and every bit of work done by anybody on any day should be done in the spirit of "liberty and justice for all." Who can state what is necessary? A head of lettuce may be much more of a necessity than a gallon of gasoline; likewise, an article from a gift shop may be much more vital to a person's happiness than a lobster dinner. Yet, some "expert planners" presume to dictate what is necessary for all of us.*

Lucy Braley Sisson became an outspoken critic of the blue laws, and in her opposition, she clearly articulated the views of many in South Middleborough, where, it was noted, "people down that way are as law abiding as anywhere. They just resent being pushed around." Despite the persuasiveness of Mrs. Sisson's arguments, most businesses without a Sunday license found it more practical to comply with the law and remain closed on Sundays. Though Williams Trading Post complied with the law, Harold Williams did admit that "the Sunday closing represented a not inconsiderable loss of business." Because many retailers along Route 28 operated during the ten-week summer season only, the loss of Sunday business was potentially economically devastating for them. The issue was largely avoided by the Middleborough Board of Selectmen, which remained generous in its issuing of Sunday retail licenses, thereby satisfying local business owners by permitting them to open. As for Lucy Braley Sisson, she was clearly ahead of her time. In 1993, Massachusetts repealed its ban on Sunday retail sales, over thirty years too late to benefit Route 28's struggling retailers.

A Business Generation Passes

With the prospect of Route 25 funneling traffic from Wareham Street and a reinvigorated enforcement of the Sunday retail blue law, South Middleborough businesses faced a gloomy prospect after the mid-1960s. Construction of the new highway was completed ahead of schedule, and the roadway was opened in its entirety on July 22, 1966. At its opening, Massachusetts governor John A. Volpe stated that the highway was an indication that "this important section of our state is not being neglected."

While southern Plymouth County may not have been being neglected per se, what in fact *was* being neglected were older communities like South Middleborough, Tremont and Wareham, which had stood along Route 28 and possessed vibrant economies at mid-century. The opening of Route 25, as anticipated, hit South Middleborough hard economically, despite all the community's best efforts to mitigate its impact. Only those businesses that had established a loyal following among local residents like Williams Trading Post and Lucy Braley's Candy Kitchen were able to weather the economic crisis. "What we are witnessing today on old Route 28 is the type of established business which will continue to operate despite being bypassed," noted the *Gazette* about the post, which it described as "a landmark in South Middleboro, [which] has a loyal following built up over the years." Despite the local newspaper's optimism, several businesses—many of them founded in the 1920s—would ultimately close, largely due to the loss of traffic associated with Route 25.

Among the older business generation at South Middleborough was Harold A. Williams (1892–1964), seen here planting peas in his garden. Williams was the founder and original owner of Williams Trading Post, which was characterized at the time of his death as "highly successful." The Trading Post is one of the few small-scale, family-owned businesses remaining in South Middleborough. *Courtesy of the Williams family.*

In 1969, Elmer Sisson sold his oil and gas business (which included the parcel on which Lucy Braley's Candy Kitchen stood) to a New Jersey–based company that immediately closed the filling station Sisson had opened in 1926. Sisson, however, stipulated that his wife be permitted to continue utilizing the Candy Kitchen building until 1974. The Candy Kitchen in fact continued to occupy the building until 1978, when, on January 24 of that year, Mrs. Sisson was given thirty days to vacate the premises. Stock on hand was donated to St. Luke's Hospital at Middleborough for the enjoyment of the patients, and eventually, the Candy Kitchen was reopened in the Sisson House on Locust Street, where it continued to operate for a few more years until Lucy Braley Sisson's death in 1983.

During this period, too, national gasoline companies that owned and operated South Middleborough's other service stations divested themselves of their interests in them as well, undoubtedly chilled by the prospect of plummeting business. In 1970, Tremarco, operator of the Houdlett's Corner station, sold the property to Edward J. Goggin, while at the opposite end of the village, Exxon (which had previously absorbed Esso) sold its station at the junction of Wareham and Spruce Streets to Henry Tinkham in 1979.

Sisson's Diner, owned by Elmer Sisson as a business venture, was, like Williams Trading Post, also able to weather the economic downturn due to the loyalty of its local clientele. One correspondent writing in 1971 was somewhat perplexed about the diner's lingering popularity. "By some standards, Sisson's Diner should not be the popular place it is. It is small, crowded, and the only air conditioning is an exhaust fan which draws off some of the heat from the grill on a warm day." Nonetheless, Sisson's was recognized as a South Middleborough institution at the time and was featured in the *Chicago Tribune*, prompting one reader to address a letter to "Tourist Bureau, South Middleboro Chamber of Commerce," which the *Gazette* found all too amusing. The diner continued to be owned throughout the period by Elmer Sisson, who declared in 1971, "As long as it's paying its way, I think I'll keep it going."

Among the restaurants operating in South Middleborough during the mid-twentieth century was Pete & Muriel's. Established in 1956 by Peter and Muriel Cammarata, the establishment operated seasonally, catering to a largely tourist-related clientele. Nonetheless, the restaurant had built a large enough local following to allow it to successfully weather the opening of Route 25.

Not so fortunate, however, were South Middleborough's other eating establishments, which, because of their seasonal operation, were more deeply affected. The Polly Pine, then known as the Polly Pine Chicken House, closed in 1968, about which time the White & Gold House also ceased operations. More successful for a time was the experience of Pete & Muriel's. This restaurant, like many of South Middleborough's businesses, operated between April and October. In 1966, undoubtedly in response to the challenge posed by the opening of Route 25, the restaurant was renovated and redecorated. An advertisement dating from August 1967 emphasized that "this spotless restaurant…continues to attract a long list of satisfied customers, in spite of the new Route 25 by-passing their establishment." Whether this was the case or mere advertising bravado is unclear. In 1976, Pete and Muriel Cammarata sold the restaurant to Norman W. and Gertrude Estabrooks of West Bridgewater, who ran the South Middleborough operation as the Estabrooks Family Restaurant until December 1984.

Similarly, the Alpine Motel closed during this period as well, hampered as it was by both the decline in traffic along Route 28 and the increasingly industrial nature of developments along the roadway, including Southeastern General Lumber, which operated a lumberyard directly across the street. The closure of the motel in the late twentieth century marked the end of an era. No longer would South Middleborough provide overnight accommodations to travelers.

TWO SOUTH MIDDLEBOROUGH INSTITUTIONS CLOSE

The decline in local business activity was mirrored in the community by the closure of two institutions that for years had helped give the South Middleborough community an identity: the South Middleborough branch library and the South Middleborough School.

In 1974, the South Middleborough branch library, which had operated in the Scout Cabin since 1941, was closed. Elinor Tompkins, Middleborough's public librarian, rationalized the closure in her report for that year:

> *The South Middleborough Branch was closed during this year and all books returned to the main library. It had become impossible to find reliable volunteers to man the library and it wasn't used enough to merit sending*

> *someone from the main library. The decision to close it was made with sadness as it had been, for many years, a busy little library.*

Though the reasons for the library's abandonment may have been entirely financial, it still disheartened the community, which once more appeared to be getting short-changed, particularly given the fact that North Middleborough was able to retain its branch library and Rock still had its own library, albeit privately operated.

More disconcerting was the closure of the South Middleborough School, which was also motivated by financial considerations and the severe fiscal challenge Middleborough faced in the late 1980s and early 1990s. As had been the case during the 1930s, when financial considerations forced the closure of the South Middleborough Railroad Station, difficult economic times would result in the permanent closure of yet another institution that had long served to provide the village with an identity.

Since nearly 1900, the South Middleborough School had been the object of the ongoing centralization of the Middleborough school system. While nine grades were originally housed in the one-classroom building, the number of grades had been whittled down, with the South Middleborough and Rock Schools (which jointly formed an informal district) housing grades one through five for the southern portion of town. Of these, the three upper grades were accommodated in South Middleborough. By 1950, the fifth grade students had been transferred to Middleborough center, and in 1952, a one-room addition was constructed on the South Middleborough School so that the third and fourth grades could be taught separately. In 1974, the fourth grade was transferred to Middleborough, and grades two and three were housed in South Middleborough, with grade one at Rock. This remained the organization until 1991.

Cognizant of the challenges faced by the two small suburban schools, Edward W. Sawicki, principal of the Southern Elementary School District (which included the Mayflower School after 1961), worked to ensure their integration into the broader school system. "In spite of the fact that these two schools are physically apart from the larger Mayflower School, attention has been focused to make them an integral part of the educational program," he noted. Nonetheless, by 1991, the existence of these schools could no longer be warranted financially, and in that year all remaining suburban schools, including South Middleborough, were permanently closed in a comprehensive rationalization that completed the centralization process begun over a century earlier. As a result, for the first time in living memory, South Middleborough was left without a school.

Residential Subdivisions

In the years following 1965, South Middleborough began to be eyed as an area ripe for residential development. Ironically, this development was partially attributable to the fact that Route 25 drew traffic from Route 28. The *Gazette* was cognizant of this development, commenting in July 1964, "Now a new trend shows evidence of developing as one notes two permits were issued for the construction of dwellings on Route 28 where once the continuous rush of traffic would have doomed such enterprise." Such development was not necessarily immediately welcomed. In December 1964, Middleborough selectmen denied the permit application of David Gregoire for the establishment of a trailer park on Wareham Street on the basis of the objections of abutters, including Herbert L. Wilber, who argued that the development would "cheapen" the neighborhood.

In 1969, a large site on Route 28 south of Houdlett's Corner was proposed for development as Massachusetts's first condominium. To be known as Leisure Towne, the community was designed for retirement age individuals. The development called for some sixteen hundred apartment units to house three thousand people. The *Middleboro Gazette* reported at the time, "Plans include a large community building, a man-made lake, recreation facilities such as a nine-hole golf course, bowling alleys, swimming pool and hobby shop." Additionally, professional offices, a hospital and shops were proposed near the site. The visionary development appears to have proved too visionary for its time. It was another twenty-five years before similar communities began to gain in popularity, and only a few of the apartment structures were ever built. Today, only one remains.

Though the small Garden Path subdivision was built at the eastern end of Pine Street, with two houses being constructed in 1977 and 1983, it was the 1990s that witnessed the largest spate of residential building in South Middleborough as subdivisions began filling the vacant land about the core of the historic center, including Katie Drive, Ridge Drive, Justine's Way, Balmy Lane and Sarah Reed Hunt Way. Pine Street, too, came in for its share of residential growth with the construction of Indian Meadow Road and Cranberry Circle following 1989 and Victorian Rose Circle in the late 1990s. Similar in scale to Indian Meadow Road was Colby Drive (with its small cul-de-sac Krista Court), which was situated off what had once been a portion of Beach Street and saw development in the 1990s.

It is likely, given the large acreage of undeveloped land in South Middleborough, that the number of residential subdivisions will multiply in the coming years. While such developments are typically well designed and neatly laid out, their recent proliferation contributes to sprawl and has the unintended effect of blurring the once familiar distinctions between Middleborough's historic villages.

Industrial Development, Zoning and the Priority Development Area

While South Middleborough was not necessarily averse to new residential construction so long as it conformed to certain standards and did not "cheapen" the neighborhood, it was less welcoming of commercial and industrial-type developments that were not in keeping with the community's character as a primarily residential community with a number of small businesses. South Middleborough, following the 1960s, in fact became an area considered by the remainder of the town as suitable for those developments not desired elsewhere, a circumstance encouraged by the general use zoning that was applied indiscriminately to South Middleborough and ultimately permitted mixed, frequently incompatible uses in what was considered by most a residential district.

In September 1962, Patrick F. O'Connor of Holbrook acquired a parcel of land on Wareham Street near Houdlett's Corner for the operation of a lumberyard. Ironically, the presence of this business was not particularly welcomed in the neighborhood, an indication of just how drastically South Middleborough's economy had turned away from lumbering since the early twentieth century. The operation of the plant, in fact, seemed to highlight the incompatibility of further industrial development with maintenance of the community's residential and small-scale business character.

Nonetheless, in 1965, when residents voiced objections to the operation of the Southeastern General lumberyard on Wareham Street, citing issues of

One of the earliest critics of the changing character of South Middleborough was Herbert L. Wilber (1890–1984), seen here in a photograph taken in 1939. Though Wilber, a lifelong resident of South Middleborough, served as a lay Methodist preacher, he was perhaps best known as Middleborough High School's Latin teacher for many years. The family was prominent at South Middleborough for four generations. *Courtesy of Middleborough Historical Association.*

noise, traffic concerns and its late-night operation, Middleborough Business and Industrial Commission chairman Kenneth Keedwell responded somewhat unsympathetically. He "emphasized the fact that the town must keep what business it can in town," implying that the concerns of South Middleborough's residents were subordinate to the needs of the town as a whole, a reiteration of the previous century's perception that South Middleborough hindered "the progress and prosperity of the old town." Yet not all agreed with Keedwell's view of the situation. When complaints regarding the same lumberyard resurfaced in early 1966, Selectman Robert L. Anderson stated, "I think this Board has gone a long way in accommodating Mr. O'Connor—a little bit too far," thereby lending credence to the South Middleborough view that a balance needed to be struck between development and maintaining the character of South Middleborough.

Just as the large undeveloped acreage at South Middleborough attracted residential property developers, so too did it catch the eye of industrial developers who required large expanses for their proposed operations. During the mid-1970s, developer Carmen Chevie acquired an extensive holding on the southwest side of the Old Colony Railroad adjacent to the Rochester town line. There he proposed a large industrial park that was derailed when Chevie was forced to file for Chapter 11 bankruptcy protection in 1976. This same property, two decades later, was designated as an "Adult Entertainment District" in a precautionary move designed to prevent the location of adult businesses in downtown Middleborough. While the likelihood of such enterprises ever establishing themselves on the South Middleborough site is extremely unlikely, the selection of the Chevie property nonetheless reinforced the link between South Middleborough and what the community regarded as undesirable development.

Similarly, in 1978, a 155-acre parcel between Route 25, Route 28 and the Beach Street extension, was considered for a demolition dump. While the Middleborough Board of Selectmen, Conservation Commission, Business and Industrial Commission, Planning Board and Police Department all supported the project, local residents did not, again highlighting the historic difference of opinion between South Middleborough and Middleborough. At a hearing before the zoning board of appeals, "local residents spent…two hours taking the plans apart piece by piece, and turning up a few things to surprise some members of the board and turn the tide against the variance," which would have permitted the project to move forward. Revealed were the facts that the dump would be designed primarily to receive refuse from urban renewal projects in Boston and Brockton, that the facility would not be run for the benefit of the town of Middleborough and, further, that the developer disclaimed any liability for possible future groundwater contamination as he proposed to turn the property over to the town once it had fulfilled its purpose.

The debate, once more, revealed the prevailing attitude outside South Middleborough, which viewed the community as an appropriate location for those types of development that were not desired elsewhere in town. Yet there was a glimmer of understanding of the South Middleborough viewpoint, as recognized by *Gazette* editor Jane Lopes:

> *At the outset of the hearing, having taken a look at a map and determined in our own head that the proposed location was out in the middle of nowhere, we took the selectmen's position that the thing was necessary and if it had to be somewhere, this was as good a place as any, better than most. That was*

> *before the hearing began. As it went on, we put ourselves in the shoes of the people who were talking about how they gave up a lot of town services and resigned themselves to having trouble getting into town and a lot of other things for the peace and quiet and open space out there in the middle of nowhere, which of course isn't the middle of nowhere if it's home.*

Though the demolition dump project failed to gain approval, South Middleborough continued to be regarded as the ideal site for development by some. Middleborough's zoning bylaws, which delineated South Middleborough as a "general use" district, open to retail, wholesale, industrial, manufacturing, warehouse, distribution, assembly, processing, fabrication, business, office and service use, simply sought to encourage development whether or not it was compatible with the residential and small business character of the district. And since no distinction was made between the historic heart of South Middleborough and the surrounding area, the possibility of large-scale industrial-type development in the center of South Middleborough became thinkable. Further fueling the fire was the Southeast Regional Planning and Economic Development District's effort to promote economic development in the district by designating South Middleborough in the late 1990s a "Priority Development Area." Though the provision of state and local tax incentives was a welcome means to stimulate economic growth within the region, no distinction was made between historic South Middleborough and its outlying districts or the types of businesses that were targeted for development. As a result, development inconsistent with South Middleborough's residential character was encouraged.

THE LOSS OF HELL'S BLAZES

The rate of change in the character of South Middleborough continued to accelerate throughout the late twentieth century as the community was increasingly loosened from its historic past, a development perhaps seen no more symbolically than in the dramatic loss of Hell's Blazes Tavern.

The tavern, long operated as a landmark restaurant catering to Cape traffic, was acquired in July 1968 by William Ekasala of Kingston, Massachusetts, and enjoyed a grand reopening on August 2, 1968. Ekesala had ambitious plans for the historic property, including the creation of "a

The former Hell's Blazes Tavern operated as a restaurant under a variety of names following 1930, including the Old Tavern and Travellers' Fare. Not until 1968 did the operation once again assume the historic Hell's Blazes name, by which it was known until its destruction by fire on May 31, 1971. Today, little remains of the once successful operation that drew visitors from near and far.

village of early American craft shops" on the property to be known as the "Tavern Shops." At the time, Hell's Blazes was stated to be the oldest tavern in America operating in its original location, and it was widely known as "a place which attracted people who consider 'going out to eat' an occasion for at least semi-formal dress; people who make dining a social ritual as well as a means of gratifying hunger. 'Gracious dining' is a term for it."

Ekasala's plans were halted when an early morning fire on May 31, 1971, leveled the kitchen and the main 1690 house, which was then serving as the dining room. Forty-five jobs were lost, and little could be salvaged save for some bricks and metal antiques that withstood the flames. In 1972, a new dining room adjoining the carriage house was constructed, and the restaurant, operated as a commercial club, sought to re-create the atmosphere of the original tavern. Owned by Frederick and Janis Dearing after 1979, Hell's Blazes continued to operate until December 31, 2003, when it closed, increasingly challenged by the opening of the Semass trash incineration plant nearly across the road in Rochester. The following year, the historic property was acquired by Costello Dismantling Company, Inc., which cleared many of the pine trees and converted the site to industrial use.

PROTECTING SOUTH MIDDLEBOROUGH'S OPEN SPACE

In contrast to the rapidly accelerating trend that regarded South Middleborough's expanses of land as suitable solely for industrial or residential development was the view that its landscape should be valued for the forests and swamps that covered it, a product of the increasingly ecologically aware 1960s. This belief prompted the most significant development in protecting South Middleborough's environment and historic landscape when seventeen hundred acres of woodland and swamp between South Middleborough and Rocky Gutter were acquired by the Commonwealth of Massachusetts for the establishment of the Rocky Gutter Wildlife Management Area in 1970.

It was perhaps fitting that the area was located near South Middleborough, which had long been recognized for the wealth of wildlife within the vicinity.

Though a resident of Highland Street in Rock, A. Whitman Higgins (1879–1961) was closely connected with South Middleborough, where he was active in the church and other organizations. A recognized amateur ornithologist in Massachusetts, he was "known throughout the area as an authority on birds and other wildlife." Higgins was also noted for his promotion of the conservation of South Middleborough's wildlife. *Courtesy of Sharon Higgins Cope-Carriere.*

The earliest settlers valued the diverse game that populated the woods, as did later hunters. During the winter of 1897–98, an unusual wagon housing two men from Campello in Brockton arrived in South Middleborough, where the men were to engage "in hunting and trapping game for the markets." The wagon, according to the Plymouth *Old Colony Memorial*, "resembled a house on wheels and bore the legend, 'Pioneer.' The interior was filled with bunks and closets and a stove was installed in one end which was fired up and smoke issued briskly from a chimney. The whole was drawn by one horse." Later, A. Whitman Higgins would have a finer appreciation for South Middleborough's wildlife, particularly its birds, acting as an amateur naturalist and ornithologist who was widely respected for his knowledge both in South Middleborough and beyond.

The land that would ultimately compose the wildlife management area was located between Wareham, Pine, France and Rocky Gutter Streets and was centered on East and West Rocky Gutter Brooks, as well as Double Brook; it had a long history of use as woodlots periodically cut by the various landowners in South Middleborough. Eventually, many of these lots were acquired by the A.D. Makepeace Company, a cranberry grower, which held the land as a watershed retention area designed to provide water for cranberry cultivation farther downstream. In 1970, the commonwealth's Division of Fisheries and Game acquired 1,541 of these acres—the single largest purchase in the division's 105-year history, which was funded by a grant of $112,525 from the Bureau of Outdoor Recreation, Department of the Interior, as well as the commonwealth's Sportsman Land Fund (created through a $1 surcharge on all hunting, fishing and trapping licenses issued in Massachusetts).

The property, a habitat for quail, grouse, snowshoe hare, cottontail rabbit, raccoon, white-tailed deer, woodcock and waterfowl, was intended as a wildlife propagation area but was to be opened to hunters. Lumbering was also intended to continue in the area, which had once been noted strictly for its woodlots. In 1998, seventy-five million board feet of white pine timber and fifty-one cords of hardwood firewood were sold from the management area. Since its original establishment, additional acreage has been added to the wildlife area, bringing the total to over three thousand acres and protecting a substantial portion of the former South Purchase and its historic uses for future generations.

SOUTH MIDDLEBOROUGH AT THE CROSSROADS

Today, South Middleborough is on the brink of its next historical era, trying to maintain its historical identity and character in the face of rapid economic and social change. In March 2002, consultants for the Massachusetts Historical Commission characterized historic South Middleborough as "highly threatened by neglect and changing land use." The general use zoning that applies to the area is likely to determine South Middleborough's future, where residences and small-scale commerce are replaced by larger, proto-industrial enterprises. This trend is already apparent in the establishment of industrial-scale businesses that have disrupted the character of the neighborhood. The presence of these concerns in the locations they occupy is compatible with neither the historic residential character nor the small commercial nature of South Middleborough. Even the historic heart of the village is likely to be threatened. In the 2003 debate over the fate of the South Middleborough schoolhouse, it was suggested that the property might be valuable as the future site of a Department of Public Works sand barn—yet one more example of a use inconsistent with the historic character of the village.

In 2001, demolition of the historic Stillman Benson House, which stood at 582 Wareham Street, and its replacement by a large-scale industrial garden operation prompted a reassessment of South Middleborough's future. A five- by two-bay, hipped-roofed, two-story Federal-style house with attached ells and an ornate mid-Victorian hood over the front center entrance, the Stillman Benson House was a noted landmark and a historic resource closely connected with the mid-nineteenth-century development of the community. Its loss was keenly felt by some within the community, so much so that overtures were made subsequently to the Middleborough Historical Commission by members of the South Middleborough Grange and South Middleborough church who were concerned by what they saw as the creeping loss of the neighborhood's character. In response, efforts were made to document and recognize the history and architecture of the South Middleborough community, including a 2002 Heritage Landscape Survey completed by the Massachusetts Department of Environmental Management. This, in turn, was followed by the nomination of South Middleborough as a historic district to the National Register of Historic Places. The nomination, prepared by Michael J. Maddigan, vice-chairman

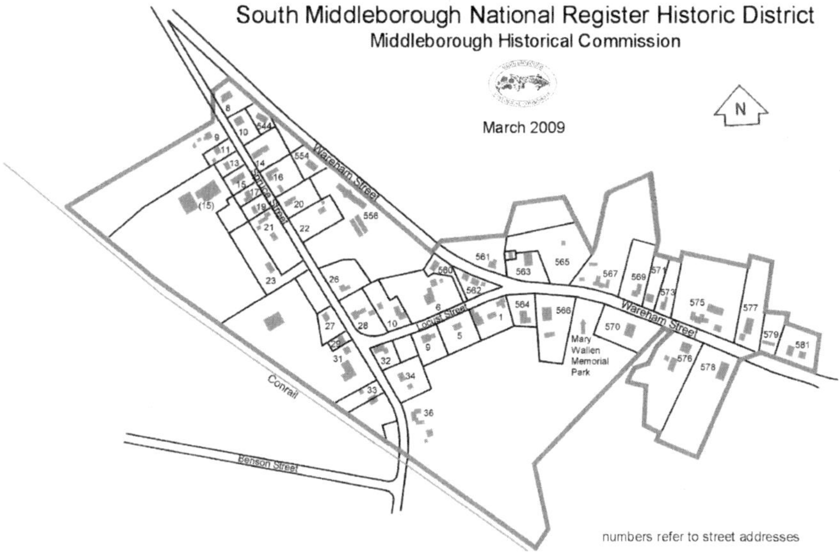

Changing land use and the loss of a number of historic resources brought about by the decline of South Middleborough's economy following 1960 prompted the 2009 listing of South Middleborough's historic core on the National Register of Historic Places. While the listing affords minimal protection for South Middleborough's cultural resources, the recognition, it is hoped, will promote greater awareness of the unique character, history and architecture of the community.

of the Middleborough Historical Commission, was approved in the summer of 2009, and South Middleborough was named as Middleborough's fourth National Register District.

Additionally, the South Middleborough Protective Association has been active in preserving the historic South Middleborough School, continuing to rehabilitate it with future plans to use it as a small museum and community center. Yet despite these gains, the losses continue. In 2008, the ancient Simeon D. Wilbur House, historically the first house encountered on the road between Middleborough and South Middleborough, was so badly gutted by fire that it was demolished the following year.

So what of the future of South Middleborough? Will it become a sprawling, commercialized strip of prefabricated buildings, paved lots and industrial uses or a small yet vibrant community of residences, small-scale commercial enterprises and revitalized historic structures? While the path is

Throughout most of its history, a strong sense of community has pervaded South Middleborough. Personal milestones such as weddings and anniversaries provided reasons for community celebrations. The twenty-fifth wedding anniversary of Herbert L. and Edith Wilber was celebrated with a picnic lunch for forty-eight guests in the rear of their home on July 2, 1939. *Courtesy of Middleborough Historical Association.*

not clear, whatever the course South Middleborough will take over the next decades, one thing is certain: the pine trees that stamp South Middleborough with an identity distinct from that of the remainder of Middleborough will likely remain, silent sentinels testifying to the community's past and watching hopefully over its future.

SOURCES

Archival Sources

Andover Newton Theological Seminary. "Records of the Third Baptist Church of Middleborough."
Library of Congress, Historic American Buildings Survey.
Massachusetts State Archives
Middleborough Historical Association. Jennie (Gammons) Phillips Hayden papers and Herbert L. Wilber papers.
Plymouth County Commissioners. "South Purchase Proprietors Records."
Plymouth County Registry of Deeds
Plymouth County Registry of Probate

Reports and Unpublished Records

Maddigan, Michael J., and Betsy Friedberg. South Middleborough National Register Nomination.
Massachusetts State Agricultural Reports
Massachusetts State Census Records
Town of Middleborough. *Annual Town Reports*, 1848–2011.
Town of Middleborough. Street listings, various.
U.S. Federal Census Records

PUBLISHED WORKS

Bliss, William Root. *Colonial Times on Buzzards Bay.* N.p., 1906.

Griffith, Henry. *History of the Town of Carver.* New Bedford, MA: E. Anthony & Sons, printers, 1913.

Lincoln, Joseph. *Thankful's Inheritance.* New York: A.L. Burt Company, 1915.

Loughlin, William G., ed. *The Diary of Isaac Backus.* Providence, RI: Brown University Press, 1979.

Peirce, Ebenezer W. "History of Middleboro." In D. Hamilton Hurd, *History of Plymouth County.* Philadelphia, PA: J.W. Lewis & Co., 1884.

Romaine, Mertie E. *History of the Town of Middleboro, Massachusetts.* Vol. II. New Bedford, MA: Reynolds-DeWalt Printing, Inc., 1969.

A Short History of the South Middleboro Methodist Church in Commemoration of the Two Hundredth Anniversary of Organized Religious Worship in South Middleboro, Massachusetts, 1761–1961. South Middleborough, MA: South Middleborough Methodist Church, 1961.

Smith, Samuel. *Memoirs of Samuel Smith, A Soldier of the Revolution, 1776–1786.* Middleborough, MA, 1853.

Weston, Thomas. *History of the Town of Middleboro, Massachusetts.* Boston: Houghton, Mifflin and Company, 1906.

NEWSPAPERS

Brockton Enterprise, Brockton, MA

Brockton Times, Brockton, MA

Middleboro Gazette, Middleborough, MA

Middleboro Gazette and Old Colony Advertiser, Middleborough, MA

Middleboro News, Middleborough, MA

Namasket Gazette, Middleborough, MA

New Bedford Standard-Times, New Bedford, MA

Old Colony Memorial, Plymouth, MA

DIRECTORIES

Crosby's Middleboro, Massachusetts Directory:1928–29. Wollaston, MA: Crosby Publishing Co., 1928.

Middleboro and Carver, Massachusetts Directory: 1934. North Hampton, NH: Crosby Publishing Co., Inc., 1934.

The Plymouth County Directory, and Historical Register of the Old Colony. Middleboro, MA: Stillman B. Pratt & Co., 1867.

Resident and Business Directory of Middleboro and Lakeville, Mass. Needham, MA: A.E. Foss & Co., 1895.

Resident and Business Directory of Middleboro and Lakeville, Mass.: 1904–5. Boston, MA: Edward A. Jones, 1904.

Resident and Business Directory of Middleboro and Lakeville, Massachusetts, For 1899. Needham, MA: A.E. Foss & Co., 1899.

Resident and Business Directory of Middleboro and Lakeville, Massachusetts: 1909. Boston, MA: Boston Suburban Book Co., 1908.

Resident and Business Directory of Middleboro, Mass. Needham, MA: Local Directory and Publishing Company, 1884.

Resident and Business Directory of Middleboro, Mass. North Cambridge, MA: Edward A. Jones, 1901.

Resident and Business Directory of Middleboro, Massachusetts: For 1897. Needham, MA: A.E. Foss & Co., 1897.

Resident and Business Directory of Middleboro, Massachusetts: 1916–1917. Boston, MA: Union Publishing Company, (Inc.), 1916.

Resident and Business Directory of Middleboro, Massachusetts: 1921–1923. Boston, MA: Union Publishing Company, 1921.

MAPS

Atlas of Plymouth County, Mass. Boston: George H. Walker & Company, 1879.

Map of Middleborough, Mass. N.p.: S. Bourne, 1831.

Map of the Town of Middleborough, Plymouth County, Mass. N.p.: H.F. Walling, 1855.

New Topographical Atlas of Surveys: Plymouth County Together with Town of Cohasset, Norfolk County, Massachusetts. Springfield, MA: The L.J. Richards Co., 1903.

INTERVIEWS

Louise (Williams) Carberry, South Middleborough, MA, 2007.
Martha (Williams) Dupuis, South Middleborough, MA, 2007.
Henry Short, Middleborough, MA, 2007.
Edward Tomasik, South Middleborough, MA, 2007.
Louise (Long) Tomasik, South Middleborough, MA, 2007.
Alma (Canova) Wilbur, Carver, MA, 2009.

INDEX

ABOUT THE AUTHOR

Michael J. Maddigan has been active in the fields of local history and historic preservation for nearly thirty years, and he currently serves as the vice-chairman of the Middleborough Historical Commission. He was responsible for the successful listing of South Middleborough on the National Register of Historic Places in 2009, much of the research for which forms the basis of *South Middleborough: A History*. His other works of local history include *Images of America: Middleborough*, *Elysian Fields: An Illustrated History of Rock Cemetery* and *Lakeville's King Philip Tavern*. He is the author of the popular local history column "Recollecting Nemasket," as well as the website of the same name.